Improving Undergraduate Education in Large Universities

Carol H. Pazandak, *Editor*
University of Minnesota

NEW DIRECTIONS FOR HIGHER EDUCATION
MARTIN KRAMER, *Editor-in-Chief*
University of California, Berkeley

Number 66, Summer 1989

Paperback sourcebooks in
The Jossey-Bass Higher Education Series

Jossey-Bass Inc., Publishers
San Francisco • London

JUL 18 1989

Carol H. Pazandak (ed.).
Improving Undergraduate Education in Large Universities.
New Directions for Higher Education, no. 66.
Volume XVII, number 2.
San Francisco: Jossey-Bass, 1989.

New Directions for Higher Education
Martin Kramer, *Editor-in-Chief*

Copyright © 1989 by Jossey-Bass Inc., Publishers
and
Jossey-Bass Limited

Copyright under International, Pan American, and Universal Copyright Conventions. All rights reserved. No part of this issue may be reproduced in any form—except for brief quotation (not to exceed 500 words) in a review or professional work—without permission in writing from the publishers.

New Directions for Higher Education is published quarterly by Jossey-Bass Inc., Publishers (publication number USPS 990-880). *New Directions* is numbered sequentially—please order extra copies by sequential number. The volume and issue numbers above are included for the convenience of libraries. Second-class postage paid at San Francisco, California, and at additional mailing offices. POSTMASTER: Send address changes to Jossey-Bass Inc., Publishers, 350 Sansome Street, San Francisco, California 94104.

Editorial correspondence should be sent to the Editor-in-Chief, Martin Kramer, 2807 Shasta Road, Berkeley, California 94708.

Library of Congress Catalog Card Number LC 85-644752
International Standard Serial Number ISSN 0271-0560
International Standard Book Number ISBN 1-55542-867-3

Cover art by WILLI BAUM
Manufactured in the United States of America. Printed on acid-free paper.

Ordering Information

The paperback sourcebooks listed below are published quarterly and can be ordered either by subscription or single copy.

Subscriptions cost $52.00 per year for institutions, agencies, and libraries. Individuals can subscribe at the special rate of $39.00 per year *if payment is by personal check*. (Note that the full rate of $52.00 applies if payment is by institutional check, even if the subscription is designated for an individual.) Standing orders are accepted.

Single copies are available at $12.95 when payment accompanies order. (California, New Jersey, New York, and Washington, D.C., residents please include appropriate sales tax.) For billed orders, cost per copy is $12.95 plus postage and handling.

Substantial discounts are offered to organizations and individuals wishing to purchase bulk quantities of Jossey-Bass sourcebooks. Please inquire.

Please note that these prices are for the calendar year 1989 and are subject to change without notice. Also, some titles may be out of print and therefore not available for sale.

To ensure correct and prompt delivery, all orders must give either the *name of an individual* or an *official purchase order number*. Please submit your order as follows:

Subscriptions: specify series and year subscription is to begin.
Single Copies: specify sourcebook code (such as, HE1) and first two words of title.

Mail orders for United States and Possessions, Latin America, Canada, Japan, Australia, and New Zealand to:
Jossey-Bass Inc., Publishers
350 Sansome Street
San Francisco, California 94104

Mail orders for all other parts of the world to:
Jossey-Bass Limited
28 Banner Street
London EC1Y 8QE

New Directions for Higher Education Series
Martin Kramer, *Editor-in-Chief*

HE1 *Facilitating Faculty Development,* Mervin Freedman
HE2 *Strategies for Budgeting,* George Kaludis
HE3 *Services for Students,* Joseph Katz

HE4   *Evaluating Learning and Teaching,* C. Robert Pace
HE5   *Encountering the Unionized University,* Jack H. Schuster
HE6   *Implementing Field Experience Education,* John Duley
HE7   *Avoiding Conflict in Faculty Personnel Practices,* Richard Peairs
HE8   *Improving Statewide Planning,* James L. Wattenbarger, Louis W. Bender
HE9   *Planning the Future of the Undergraduate College,* Donald G. Trites
HE10 *Individualizing Education by Learning Contracts,* Neal R. Berte
HE11 *Meeting Women's New Educational Needs,* Clare Rose
HE12 *Strategies for Significant Survival,* Clifford T. Stewart, Thomas R. Harvey
HE13 *Promoting Consumer Protection for Students,* Joan S. Stark
HE14 *Expanding Recurrent and Nonformal Education,* David Harman
HE15 *A Comprehensive Approach to Institutional Development,* William Bergquist, William Shoemaker
HE16 *Improving Educational Outcomes,* Oscar Lenning
HE17 *Renewing and Evaluating Teaching,* John A. Centra
HE18 *Redefining Service, Research, and Teaching,* Warren Bryan Martin
HE19 *Managing Turbulence and Change,* John D. Millett
HE20 *Increasing Basic Skills by Developmental Studies,* John E. Roueche
HE21 *Marketing Higher Education,* David W. Barton, Jr.
HE22 *Developing and Evaluating Administrative Leadership,* Charles F. Fisher
HE23 *Admitting and Assisting Students After Bakke,* Alexander W. Astin, Bruce Fuller, Kenneth C. Green
HE24 *Institutional Renewal Through the Improvement of Teaching,* Jerry G. Gaff
HE25 *Assuring Access for the Handicapped,* Martha Ross Redden
HE26 *Assessing Financial Health,* Carol Frances, Sharon L. Coldren
HE27 *Building Bridges to the Public,* Louis T. Benezet, Frances W. Magnusson
HE28 *Preparing for the New Decade,* Larry W. Jones, Franz A. Nowotny
HE29 *Educating Learners of All Ages,* Elinor Greenberg, Kathleen M. O'Donnell, William Bergquist
HE30 *Managing Facilities More Effectively,* Harvey H. Kaiser
HE31 *Rethinking College Responsibilities for Values,* Mary Louise McBee
HE32 *Resolving Conflict in Higher Education,* Jane E. McCarthy
HE33 *Professional Ethics in University Administration,* Ronald H. Stein, M. Carlota Baca
HE34 *New Approaches to Energy Conservation,* Sidney G. Tickton
HE35 *Management Science Applications to Academic Administration,* James A. Wilson
HE36 *Academic Leaders as Managers,* Robert H. Atwell, Madeleine F. Green
HE37 *Designing Academic Program Reviews,* Richard F. Wilson
HE38 *Successful Responses to Financial Difficulties,* Carol Frances
HE39 *Priorities for Academic Libraries,* Thomas J. Galvin, Beverly P. Lynch
HE40 *Meeting Student Aid Needs in a Period of Retrenchment,* Martin Kramer
HE41 *Issues in Faculty Personnel Policies,* Jon W. Fuller
HE42 *Management Techniques for Small and Specialized Institutions,* Andrew J. Falender, John C. Merson
HE43 *Meeting the New Demand for Standards,* Jonathan R. Warren
HE44 *The Expanding Role of Telecommunications in Higher Education,* Pamela J. Tate, Marilyn Kressel
HE45 *Women in Higher Education Administration,* Adrian Tinsley, Cynthia Secor, Sheila Kaplan

HE46 *Keeping Graduate Programs Responsive to National Needs,* Michael J. Pelczar, Jr., Lewis C. Solomon
HE47 *Leadership Roles of Chief Academic Officers,* David G. Brown
HE48 *Financial Incentives for Academic Quality,* John Folger
HE49 *Leadership and Institutional Renewal,* Ralph M. Davis
HE50 *Applying Corporate Management Strategies,* Roger J. Flecher
HE51 *Incentive for Faculty Vitality,* Roger G. Baldwin
HE52 *Making the Budget Process Work,* David J. Berg, Gerald M. Skogley
HE53 *Managing College Enrollments,* Don Hossler
HE54 *Institutional Revival: Case Histories,* Douglas W. Steeples
HE55 *Crisis Management in Higher Education,* Hal Hoverland, Pat McInturff, C. E. Tapie Rohm, Jr.
HE56 *Managing Programs for Learning Outside the Classroom,* Patricia Senn Breivik
HE57 *Creating Career Programs in a Liberal Arts Context,* Mary Ann F. Rehnke
HE58 *Financing Higher Education: Strategies After Tax Reform,* Richard E. Anderson, Joel W. Meyerson
HE59 *Student Outcomes Assessment: What Institutions Stand to Gain,* Diane F. Halpern
HE60 *Increasing Retention: Academic and Student Affairs Administrators in Partnership,* Martha McGinty Stodt, William M. Klepper
HE61 *Leaders on Leadership: The College Presidency,* James L. Fisher, Martha W. Tack
HE62 *Making Computers Work for Administrators,* Kenneth C. Green, Steven W. Gilbert
HE63 *Research Administration and Technology Transfer,* James T. Kenny
HE64 *Successful Strategic Planning: Case Studies,* Douglas W. Steeples
HE65 *The End of Mandatory Retirement: Effects on Higher Education,* Karen C. Holden, W. Lee Hansen

Contents

Editor's Notes 1
Carol H. Pazandak

1. **Surviving Institutional Change: Reflections on Curriculum Reform in Universities** 9
Karen Seashore Louis
Institutionalized curriculum change requires administrative leaders in key positions as "lead mediators" and change agents.

2. **Research and Assessment: Tools for Change** 27
Warren W. Willingham
Good research ideas do not come easily, but when wisely used, they will clarify questions, force issues, rationalize debate, vitalize the change process, and justify new departures.

3. **Pathways to Success: Transforming Obstacles into Opportunities** 41
Joan B. Garfield, Darwin D. Hendel
Pilot projects at program levels serve as indicators that each faculty and staff member can make a difference.

4. **Achieving Excellence: How Will We Know?** 51
Clifton F. Conrad, David J. Eagan
A successful university plan to monitor and evaluate change recognizes the need to involve all stakeholders in the planning and implementation process.

5. **Seeking Coherence in the Curriculum** 65
Joan S. Stark
Building coherent programs is the real challenge to better undergraduate education.

6. **Undergraduate Curriculum 2000** 77
Arthur Levine
The time is ripe for change, and universities under bold leadership can learn from the past in charting the future.

Appendix. Framework for a Workshop on Good Practice in Undergraduate Education 85
Arthur W. Chickering

Index 89

Editor's Notes

This sourcebook addresses major issues in planning for improvements in undergraduate education at large, comprehensive, research universities. The changing demographics of the U.S. population, the growth and change of higher education nationally, and the national wave of concern about the quality of education set the context.

Today's large, comprehensive, research universities achieve excellence through faculty reputations in publications and research, levels of grant activity, and the accomplishments of their doctoral graduates. But no major American university could survive without the presence of substantial numbers of undergraduates. Further, public universities have an obligation defined by mission and funding to provide undergraduate education to the state's citizens; in fact, they award more than half of the nation's baccalaureate degrees annually. The challenge to serve all masters in this environment can lead to the neglect of this least powerful and knowledgeable of the university's constituencies.

The resources of a comprehensive institution, offering professional and graduate study and a faculty engaged in research, afford unique opportunities to undergraduates. The potential for students to find a match for their educational needs, interests, and aptitudes is excellent. At the same time, the complexity of a comprehensive university creates special challenges in providing undergraduate education. The issues that need to be addressed are who shall be educated, what shall comprise that education, and how shall it be provided. A parallel issue is that of assessment for the purposes of improvement and accountability. How will the university document the quality of its undergraduate education? How will it improve those aspects of its educational programs and services found wanting? Finally, should a public university that has tried to be all things to all people focus and narrow its aim?

Concerns for effective teaching and successful learning are common in all institutions of higher education, but communication among students, faculty, and administration is more diffuse and difficult to achieve in large institutions. The initiation of change and the drive to implement, sustain, and evaluate it face constant pressures from other demands on faculty and staff. The structure of the institution creates a governance system that can undermine any centrally mandated change strategy. At the same time, the chief academic administrators are crucial in setting policies and developing institutional attitudes. Because of sheer size, more resources are available, but competition for them is keen, and more steps exist between allocation and expenditure. Reward structures, perhaps the most powerful determinants of individual faculty behavior, have rarely been directed toward undergraduate education.

Examples of Successful Institutional Change

Several recent national examples of change efforts have already become legend in higher education circles. Alverno College (Alverno College Faculty, 1985a, 1985b) offers an example of an internally mandated plan founded on institutional educational objectives. The disparate natures of a small, private, vocationally oriented college for women and an enormous comprehensive public university argue against the direct transferability of the model. But the idea that an institution should define whom it is to educate, how and for what goals, and how it will assess outcomes is eminently transferable. Alverno serves as a model for those who wish to focus on student development by creating an atmosphere that encourages individual talents and that incorporates ongoing formative evaluation strategies to aid the teaching and student learning process.

External mandates from the state to improve education are increasingly common today and are frequently tied to funding. Two thirds of the states in the nation are now calling for some form of institutional evaluation that shows accountability (Boyer, Ewell, Finney, and Mingle, 1987). The Education Commission of the States (1986) has called for a broader state-level role in improving undergraduate education. The experiment at the University of Tennessee at Knoxville, encouraged by the funding program of the state's Higher Education Commission (Banta and Fisher, 1984; Banta, 1985), is an example of a large institution shaping its programs initially to gain budgeting bonuses but then moving on to make major modifications in curriculum and instruction. Such external pressures raise an important set of accountability issues different from those faced by Alverno College. In contrast with Alverno's internally driven evaluation based on the individual student's academic and personal development, external demands for accountability focus on institutional characteristics, particularly in comparisons with peer universities. Comparisons in terms of program accreditation and student test scores on entering and leaving clearly indicate an institution's standing among peers; changes over time in these indicators represent growth or decline for the institution, and when acted on can have a beneficial effect on the undergraduate student experience. Such external forces serve two major functions: They engender legitimate external accountability, and they encourage internal efforts to be more responsive to undergraduate education programs.

Commitment to Focus: The Minnesota Experience

Much of this volume springs from an effort to assess the progress of and prospects for curricular improvement at a third institution—the University of Minnesota. In May 1988, a conference brought together a number of people from the university and several scholars known nationally for their concern with curricular reform and the management of change in higher education. This sourcebook combines their reflections on the national experience and the generalizable aspects of the Minnesota experience. The Appendix presents the framework for a workshop on good practices in higher education that was used to promote discussion at the conference.

The chronicle of the University of Minnesota's efforts to improve undergraduate teaching and learning exemplifies the difficulties that large and complex universities face in trying to meet the challenge to improve. *A Commitment to Focus,* a document written in February 1985 by then interim President Kenneth Keller (1985), set the process in motion. It synthesized the outcomes of a ten-year university planning process and was, in part, a response to the governor's request that each higher education system in the state clarify and differentiate its mission. It was also designed to set the tone for the new administration of the university. The document, receiving, on balance, positive response from the university faculty as well as from the external community, nevertheless became one more force leading to the early termination of Keller's presidency. The plan also evoked charges of elitism in a highly populist state, in part because it was not fully articulated and thus was subject to misunderstanding.

Minnesota has three separately governed higher education systems, including the university with its major campus in the Twin Cities metropolitan area of over 2 million residents and with four smaller campuses located across the state; a seven-campus state university system; and an eighteen-campus community college system. Although these systems have defined missions, the differences among them have been less than exact. As a state land-grant institution and the oldest and largest public university in the state, the University of Minnesota has always held undergraduate education to be a major responsibility. During recent decades, the strong community college system and the increasingly comprehensive set of state universities have begun to provide excellent public alternatives to the university. The time had come to recognize and adapt to these changes in opportunity. The university, in its new commitment, set as its target to become one of the top five public research institutions in the country. This target included excellence in all areas within its missions, among them undergraduate education. In exchange for limiting the number of undergraduates, and specifically the number of entering freshmen, the university intended to provide the best education possible for those undergraduates whom it enrolled. *A Commitment to Focus* was a general statement of intent addressing the multiple roles of the university. The specific recipe for a good undergraduate education and how the institution was to move ahead were left to be discovered in subsequent discussions.

Four major barriers to the realization of "the full potential of undergraduate education" on campus were identified by one blue-ribbon committee, the Implementation Task Force on Undergraduate Education (1987). These barriers exemplify the problems rampant in large universities and were formative in planning the conference that gave rise to this sourcebook:

1. Absence of a sense of community—The size and increasing diversity of the student body, its commuter nature, and the fact that most students work off campus to finance their education make it difficult to form learning communities and to identify with the university.

2. Insufficient integration of the curriculum—With too many courses to choose from and too little guidance in selecting them, students may find themselves with fragmented and incoherent degree programs.

3. Insufficient clarity of purpose—The educational experiences provided to students have lacked clear goal statements, making it impossible for the university to assess the outcomes of those experiences.

4. Uneven attention to teaching—Efforts to encourage and reward undergraduate teaching have not been institutionalized. Clearer definitions of good teaching, better evaluation, and stronger incentives and support for the improvement of teaching are needed.

Identifying the Elements of Excellence. An opening conference panel of faculty, students, and administrators identified keys to improving undergraduate education. The four most pertinent elements are the following:

1. *Attend to the individual student as learner.* This has two components: awareness of and accommodation to the broad range of individual differences among students in terms of learning styles and preparation, and awareness of university expectations for learning so that students can make wise choices about enrollment and programs of study.

2. *Recognize that research and scholarly work are fundamental to the faculty role and should infuse the content and methods of teaching.* Classrooms then become apprentice laboratories, and students learn how knowledge is gained. They should be encouraged to put knowledge and skills together in internships and other endeavors outside the classroom. An important aspect of the discovery process is the confrontation of different ideas and scholarly opinions so that students understand the changing nature of scholarly knowledge both within and between disciplines.

3. *Design undergraduate education to provide important knowledge, values, and general skills that will facilitate lifelong learning.* The task of the faculty is to train generalists at the undergraduate level who will bring their education to work in society. The curriculum should be guided by three objectives: the provision of a general knowledge and skills base; the enhancement of individual student abilities, interests, and values; and the awareness of the diversity and interdependence of today's world. To this end, faculty must work across disciplines to provide courses more appropriate for generalists.

4. *Avoid a graduate education model at the undergraduate level.* A major deterrent to providing an outstanding undergraduate education arises from the disciplinary or research orientation of the institution. Training graduate students to follow in faculty footsteps comes naturally. Specialized disciplinary knowledge and development of research skills suit an apprentice model well. Undergraduate education, however, has other objectives that will prepare students for twenty-first century careers. These objectives are based on the conviction that the development of individual abilities is primary and the acquisition of specific knowledge follows.

Identifying the Facets of Change. Fostering fundamental changes in educational programs and practices is a monumental project that requires high visibility at the top, commitment of energy and resources, a long lead time, and instructional and support staff that are convinced of the value of the changes and of their own abilities to implement them.

The authors of chapters in this sourcebook repeatedly and independently identify common problems in making and monitoring change at large, complex universities. One problem is the nature of the institutional structure, which is characterized by "departmental independence, diffused leadership, and unclear channels of accountability" (see Chapter Four). This structure adds a dimension to planning, implementation, and evaluation that is qualitatively different from the change process at smaller, single-purpose, or at least, less complex colleges. The program and faculty diversity inherent in a comprehensive university also makes a difference in the change process. Divergent visions of a liberal education arise from differing disciplinary perspectives and are further complicated by the press of professional programs. Planning for change requires an understanding that the process of discovery is fundamental if the product is to be accepted. Developing consensus is likely to be long and arduous, but it is essential if a set of common objectives or a common core program is to be activated successfully. Further, discovery is an experience unique to each individual. Fertilization of views across disciplinary and collegiate boundaries must be an ongoing process if a common vision is to be defined and embraced.

Designing undergraduate education for the next decades goes beyond a sense of mission, beyond curricular and program requirements, and beyond consensus. It means improving the teaching and learning process. Arthur Chickering and Zelda Gamson (1987) have used "Seven Principles for Good Practice in Undergraduate Education" to elicit faculty, student, and administrative perceptions in a workshop format. These principles are derived from decades of research on learning and teaching but have not yet found their way into the behavioral norms of the typical university and college.

To bring about change, individual faculty members must engage in the process. They are the developers and implementers of curricular and instructional changes. The impact of these classroom-level changes on the greater environment of the institution depends on communication of the developments, yet communication within large research institutions has proved to be exceedingly difficult. Innovative examples operate in relative isolation from one another and outside of general campus awareness. Many aspects of these special programs could be generalized to benefit the total educational environment, but this process requires central leadership and commitment. Top administrators must provide the overarching vision and continuing encouragement and support that will foster change efforts, will determine that the changes have a positive impact, and will help to create a shared awareness of changes, all the while ensuring that the locus of control for ideas and developments remains at the unit level. It is a nice feat to balance central support and oversight of direction with collegiate and faculty control of the changes themselves. Yet the nature of a large, complex university indicates that other strategies are unlikely to work.

Summary

When a comprehensive institution sets forth to attend to undergraduate education, the prospects for improving student learning afforded by the enormous resources of a large research faculty are tantalizing. But improving undergraduate education is not a process to be undertaken lightly. It is arduous, and failure has serious implications. Real improvement requires more than tinkering. A sense of vision regarding objectives is essential, yet the process of discovering the vision and articulating it can take a long time. In short, an institutional commitment to change will arise only from widely perceived discrepancies between what is and what ought to be.

Organization of This Sourcebook

This sourcebook grew out of a conference on improving undergraduate education through research and practice that was held at the University of Minnesota on May 6 and 7, 1988. Several authors of chapters in this sourcebook were invited speakers at the conference, and their chapters are based on their conference presentations. The intent of the sourcebook is to bring together the major issues that large universities face as they seek to improve undergraduate education.

In Chapter One, Karen Seashore Louis outlines approaches to change management and survival, using as an example the *Commitment to Focus* document and the impact it has had on the University of Minnesota. She provides support for her thesis that, in a complex university of semiautonomous collegiate units, a theme or vision that challenges a response from colleges and departments is more likely to result in change than a set of objectives fixed by the university's central administration.

In Chapter Two, Warren W. Willingham reviews the uses of research and assessment in educational change. Many external forces that mold higher education, such as Sputnik and the GI Bill, have elicited institutional response, but related research is primarily for monitoring. However, an internal process of ongoing institutional renewal can make the best use of assessment in support of useful change. Willingham discusses the characteristics required for an assessment program to remain vital to the educational planning process as well as to help the institution respond to external change.

Chapter Three by Joan B. Garfield and Darwin D. Hendel provides examples of innovative faculty projects to improve undergraduate education. Selected University of Minnesota-Twin Cities faculty presented these research-based projects at the conference in May 1988 both to share their findings and to encourage others to follow suit.

In Chapter Four, Clifton F. Conrad and David J. Eagan review models and strategies for assessment to answer the question: How will an institution know if it has reached its targets for change? They discuss issues critical to the design of a useful assessment program. The assessment methods will vary with the specific purposes for assessment and may change over time, but any successful assessment program requires that the users understand, accept, and join in the evaluation process.

Chapter Five by Joan S. Stark is a hypothetical case study of a cross-disciplinary university faculty committee engaged in the task of designing a core course. The basis for her case study is her extensive knowledge of discipline differences in faculty attitudes toward the curriculum. These differences, strikingly apparent in a large, complex institution, add a dimension to planning that the administration must reckon with if change is to occur.

In Chapter Six, Arthur Levine discusses objectives for an undergraduate curriculum in a complex university as we approach the twenty-first century. He cites examples from the past as guidance for today. The present is a period of rapid social change and requires response to dimly understood forces. If the university is to emerge as a strong and vibrant institution, it must determine which educational needs of society it intends to meet and, therefore, how it will prepare its students.

The Appendix, by Arthur W. Chickering, contains an outline for a faculty workshop on improving the teaching and learning process. Chickering conducted a successful workshop using this outline as part of the May 1988 conference at the University of Minnesota.

Carol H. Pazandak
Editor

References

Alverno College Faculty. *Assessment at Alverno College.* (Rev. ed.) Milwaukee, Wisc.: Alverno Productions, 1985a.
Alverno College Faculty. *Liberal Learning at Alverno College.* (Rev. ed.) Milwaukee, Wisc.: Alverno Productions, 1985b.
Banta, T. W. (ed.). *Performance Funding in Higher Education: A Case Study.* Boulder, Colo.: National Center for Higher Education Management Systems, 1985.
Banta, T. W., and Fisher, H. S. "Performance Funding: Tennessee's Experiment." In J. K. Folger (ed.), *Financial Incentives for Academic Quality.* New Directions for Higher Education, no. 48. San Francisco: Jossey-Bass, 1984.
Boyer, C. M., Ewell, P. T., Finney, J. E., and Mingle, J. R. "Assessment and Outcomes Measurement: A View from the States." *AAHE Bulletin,* 1987, *39* (7), 8-12.
Chickering, A. W., and Gamson, Z. F. "Seven Principles for Good Practice in Undergraduate Education." *AAHE Bulletin,* 1987, *39* (7), 2-7.
Education Commission of the States. *Transforming the State Role in Undergraduate Education: Time for a Different View.* Report no. PS-86-3. Denver, Colo.: Education Commission of the States, 1986.
Implementation Task Force on Undergraduate Education on the Twin Cities Campus of the University of Minnesota. *Final Report.* Minneapolis: University of Minnesota, 1987.
Keller, K. *A Commitment to Focus: Report of Interim President Kenneth H. Keller to the Board of Regents.* Minneapolis: University of Minnesota, 1985.

Carol H. Pazandak is associate professor in counseling psychology and the College of Liberal Arts Collegewide Programs, University of Minnesota.

Educational changes require attention to system and organizational characteristics, as well as the development of networks of interpersonal influences.

Surviving Institutional Change: Reflections on Curriculum Reform in Universities

Karen Seashore Louis

Observers of universities are more often struck by the stability of these institutions than by their adaptability. The management literature usually assumes that organizations make major changes largely as a consequence of negative feedback from the environment. Unlike most for-profit and nonprofit organizations that have clearer indicators of their relative success in the market, large institutions of higher education often seem to walk almost to the abyss before they recognize the need to change. This does not mean that they are somnolent or lack dynamism; many shifts and alterations in the way a university does things occur every year. Yet these often do not add up to institutional change; rather, they merely patch up the existing system.

I would like to thank the participants in my graduate research seminar for stimulating the thoughts that led to this chapter: Anne Auten, Shelley Diment, Leo Krzywkowski, Jayne Larsen, Dean Schieve, Jan Schleuter, Mary Van Voorhis, Steve Watson, and Carol Werdin.

During a recent graduate research seminar, several students and I tried to understand the dynamics of planned change in universities by examining the "Commitment to Focus" effort (hereafter called "Focus") at the University of Minnesota. "Focus" was based on a strategic planning process that attempted to narrow the mission of the university in order to improve the quality of undergraduate education and the university's standing among major research institutions.

As part of our seminar, we reviewed piles of documents, engaged in extended discussions with key administrators, and interviewed department chairs and faculty members in several colleges. The seminar examined many aspects of "Focus" (and was enlivened in the middle of the quarter by the resignation of the university president, the major architect of the change effort), but, in this chapter, I will emphasize lessons that can be drawn for the management of curriculum reform in large and complex institutions of higher education. These lessons will be summarized in the form of propositions for surviving change.

The Braid of Institutional Change

Current discussions about needed changes in undergraduate education are usually based on what Tichy (1980) calls the "technical design problem" of change. Such discussions are concerned with defining what is taught to whom, the desired learning results, the financial resources necessary to achieve change, and the needed leadership support inside the university. Thus, for example, "Focus" documents emphasized the need to add faculty and resources in critical areas; to restructure admission procedures and lower-division offerings; to improve advising, increase admission requirements, and reduce the number of undergraduates; and to restructure the use of time by lengthening class periods and moving from a quarter to a semester system (Keller, 1985; University of Minnesota, 1986).

Tichy points out, however, that organizational problems (and solutions) are never merely technical; they are also political and cultural. By political, I mean that a significant effort to reform undergraduate education has implications for both the distribution of resources between units and divisions and the overall patterns of influence within the university. At the University of Minnesota, for example, suggestions about having a single point of entry into the university for freshmen were resisted in the Institute of Technology, where science, math, and engineering departments are located. This resistance was motivated by the desire of the faculty and dean to control the admission and curriculum experiences of their majors. Similarly, there was opposition to the proposal to split the very large College of Liberal Arts into two smaller colleges. Some faculty in departments designated for the College of Humanities expressed concern about ending up as financial "have-nots" if they were forced to compete directly with a College of Social Studies. The latter would have a richer resource base of grants and national prestige, since "Focus" proposed to reallocate resources to middle-ranked departments that were strong but not in the top five in the country.

Cultural problems arose because of value differences among faculty and between faculty and administrators regarding undergraduate education. Thus, for example, there were concerns about "Focus" language that justified the proposed changes in terms of their utility to the state's economy. Quite a few saw this as an elitist bias toward technical and scientific education that undermined the historic liberal arts function of universities. Others objected because they saw a need to be more sensitive to the origins of the university as a land-grant institution and advocated a broader admission policy. These two value themes are not, of course, unique to Minnesota and the 1980s but have characterized debates over the goals of higher education in the U.S. since the 1860s (Brubacher and Rudy, 1976).

These factors lead to a proposition for surviving change:

Proposition 1: Management of change in universities requires attention to the braid of technical, political, and cultural problems and of technical, political, and cultural consequences of the solutions that are offered to address these problems.

Furthermore, the balance of technical, political, and cultural problems in the institution will affect the best approach to change management and survival. This balance is not predictable, except in the very short term, and the longer and more comprehensive the institutional change process, the more likely it will shift, demanding different approaches to the survival and protection of the change efforts.

The implications of this and other propositions will be explored in the rest of the chapter. First I will look at the organizational characteristics of universities and how they affect change. Then I will look briefly at the "Focus" process as an illustration of how key actors affect the curriculum change process. Finally, I will offer some research-based suggestions about managing and surviving large-scale institutional change.

Institutional Characteristics That Influence Change

To be an overt or covert change agent within an institution requires some insight into the U.S. higher education system. Let me frame this as a second proposition:

Proposition 2: To understand how to survive the change process, we must understand the organizational features of the setting in which change occurs. The most critical are the higher education system, the institution, and the college or department in which the reform is being carried out.

The Higher Education System. A recent article by Trow (1988) summarizes the salient features of the U.S. system of higher education in comparison with other developed countries. Here, I will elaborate on their implications for the undergraduate curriculum.

Market Driven. The U.S. system gives primacy to consumer control. Even public universities are financed through enrollment capitation, and student choices largely govern enrollment. Decisions by both state and federal government to subsidize higher education indirectly through student grants and loans undergird this characteristic.

Thus, unlike most European countries, where changes in undergraduate education are negotiated by the government or the professoriat, we can only consider revisions that will be acceptable to potential students. Consumer influence over the curriculum occurs in elite as well as less selective universities (Manns and March, 1978).

Designed for Consumer Flexibility. We are part of an institutionally diverse system that is designed to be flexible for students. Public and private institutions have variable admission standards, program offerings, and the number and types of degrees offered. In addition, the system has evolved to permit students to move between institutions with ease. Each year fewer students start college at one institution and complete their degree four years later at the same institution. Students even enroll at two institutions simultaneously in order to balance the desire for prestige with tuition breaks or other factors. A system that is flexible for the individual student, however, produces rigidity when it comes to reforming undergraduate education. First, undergraduate programs must all look alike in certain ways. With very few exceptions, units (courses) are required to have titles and a departmental base that are recognizable to other institutions. Second, an emphasis on cumulative learning is difficult except in fields where there is disciplinary consensus on the sequential ordering of concepts and skills. Only a few small, private institutions can vary much from the mold.

Strong Administration, Weak Professoriat. The conventional view is that faculty control the curriculum and instruction process. In fact, compared with other countries, our faculties are relatively uninfluential, and administrators at all levels have a lot of influence (Baldridge, Curtis, Ecker, and Riley, 1978). Collectively, professors lack the stature to influence public perceptions of what the curriculum should be; former Secretary of Education William Bennett or Harvard President Derek Bok has more influence on public opinion than the faculties of Stanford or Harvard. More important, professors do not control the allocation of resources and therefore do not determine the importance (or ranking) of undergraduate educational programs relative to one another.

The somewhat painful implication from the faculty's perspective is that systemwide reform of undergraduate education involves administrators (and policy makers) as well as faculty. Faculty may dominate (or successfully resist) the process, but they will not exclusively control its shape.

Lay Control. U.S. higher education is unique in the influence of laypersons over policy. While this holds for both private and public universities, the boards of public universities usually represent major state constituencies rather than an elite. At the University of Minnesota, as at other public universities, the regents acted as a brake against perceived elitism during "Focus," as those representing a populist thrust argued with those wishing to "focus" the university position as a dominant research institution with selective undergraduate education.

Other outside groups may control the curriculum both directly (through lobbying) and indirectly (through preventing resource reallocations within the university). The public reaction to "Focus" efforts to close or cut specific graduate professional schools provides a case in point: Numerous public actors argued (usually successfully) for the value of every program designated for budget reductions in order to reallocate funds to undergraduate education.

The implication is that it is not possible—and is probably not desirable in terms of overall institutional effectiveness—to follow Peters and Waterman's (1982) suggestion to "stick to the knitting" and emphasize an undergraduate curriculum based on a classical liberal arts and science model (or any other single approach). It is undesirable because, in public and publicly regulated institutions, a narrow focus may undermine support from critical constituencies and may therefore threaten survival (Snow and Hrebiniek, 1980). In this regard, even large private universities are, to a great extent, publicly regulated because of their dependence on federal grants and student loan policies.

Organizational Characteristics of the Large University. Recent literature on major changes in institutions of higher education has emphasized smaller colleges and universities. The problem of managing and surviving change, however, is different in institutions of varying size and complexity. A critical distinction between large and smaller or private institutions is in internal diversity (Kerr, 1964).

Students. The large university has a more diverse student body than most other institutions. At the University of California, Berkeley, for example, there are now more ethnic minority students than Caucasians; at the University of Minnesota, the average undergraduate is in his or her midtwenties. In consequence, it is difficult to define a clear market for the institution's curriculum—or even for a specific course. While some diversity is stimulating in a class, we deal with a range of student backgrounds and experience that makes it difficult to design elegant or even coherent models for the curriculum.

Faculty. Faculty in these settings cannot form a collegium. They may divide into clear interest groups; Kerr (1964) talks about the "scientists affluent, humanists militant" syndrome. Many faculty isolate themselves from governance outside of their own departments and do not view themselves as engaged in a university-wide enterprise of undergraduate education. There is no body that brings all undergraduate faculty together, and different departmental cultures emerge as a consequence.

Thus, efforts to restructure the undergraduate curriculum may promote overt conflict and competition among different sectors of the university. At the University of Minnesota, rather than concentrating energy on a clear educational mission, "Focus" raised value (and resource allocation) disputes that had been hidden below the surface.

Resources. Although a university's budget is enrollment driven, a significant percentage of the budget at many universities does come from external research or program grants. Since grants determine the power of departments in the budgeting process (Pfeffer and Salancik, 1982; Pfeffer and Moore, 1980), funding agencies exert an indirect influence over department expansion and, therefore, over curriculum. Furthermore, as Kerr (1964) pointed out, this increasing emphasis on external funding has changed the institutional focus from undergraduate to graduate instruction. Serious alternative incentives would have to be applied to get faculty with strong ties to external funding agencies to emphasize the broad needs of undergraduate education.

Summary of Consequences for Undergraduate Reform. Universities exist in a political environment composed of shifting internal and external coalitions (Baldridge, Curtis, Ecker, and Riley, 1978). Compared with simpler institutions and previous times, both the president and the faculty at large universities are less powerful (Kerr, 1964). March and his colleagues describe the university at different times as ambiguous (Cohen and March, 1974) and a "garbage can of solutions, problems, and people" (March and Olsen, 1986). The university also has a weak institutional culture and is organized around clans (departments). There is little agreement on goals and means, and different parts of the university operate independently from each other (Weick, 1976). Each institution is part of a larger system of U.S. education and other universities. Radical change in one institution (for example, changing the tenure system to give more weight to teaching) is difficult without concurrent changes in the larger context.

Leadership for Curriculum Reform

The preceding discussion leads to a third proposition:

Proposition 3: Ambiguity of leadership, combined with rigidities in the social environment and the politically loaded internal environment, creates a leadership vacuum at the top with regard to curriculum reform.

Who is to take charge? How can reform come about, even on a nonradical scale?

Role of the Central Administration. To illustrate the difference between large and small institutions, we may contrast the recently described case of Antioch University (Taylor, 1987) with the University of Minnesota's "Commitment to Focus." Within two years, Antioch's President Guskin was able to close several branches and cut the budgets of others in order to shift the institution's central emphasis back to undergraduate liberal arts at the Yellow Springs campus. The board, alumni, faculty, and students rallied behind his dramatic actions. At the University of Minnesota, in contrast, the planning and change process initiated by Kenneth Keller has taken more than seven years and has met massive resistance both inside and out. The goals were similar; many of the proposed actions were the same; most would agree that both Keller and Guskin were visionary leaders; most would also agree that both institutions were in drastic need of some improvement. What differed most significantly was the institutional context.

Let us look more closely at "Focus" as a stimulus for curriculum change. This is not a critique of "Focus." Rather, the major point I wish to make is that "Focus" was a centrally initiated plan to clarify the role of the university in relation to other state educational systems and in regard to its public service obligations on a state and national level. This proposal for strategic adaptation between the university and its external context is different from a plan for reforming undergraduate education. In "Focus," the two processes have been, up to now, largely unrelated in practice (although they have been verbally linked).

Although "Focus" has been characterized as "bold and visionary," it initially contained something for everyone, consistent with the need to satisfy both internal and external constituencies. On the one hand, it emphasized the need to reallocate resources to improve undergraduate education and used the demonstrable decline in the quality of undergraduate education as a means of mustering support among various constituencies in the state. On the other hand, another "Focus" goal—"bringing the university into the top five"—generated faculty support among departments concerned about their inability to hire "the best and the brightest" due to declining salaries and equipment.

"Focus" thus operated on an implicit "trickle-down" theory of reform in undergraduate education: Increased resources, including faculty, would create a better educational environment in general, which would be supplemented by additional resources in those areas of high faculty load and poor student-faculty ratios. When it came to the details of undergraduate reform, a college-level planning process was intended to stimulate departments to consider curriculum, but how this was to happen was a "black box." The *Guidelines to the College* (University of Minnesota, 1986) does not mention curriculum review, although colleges were cautioned to remember that "undergraduate programs should emphasize intellectual engagement, social awareness, ethical involvement, and participation in an intellectual community. . . . The idea that education is a continuum should underlie each college plan" (p. 3).

Interviews with fifteen department chairs, however, lead to the conclusion that this indirect stimulus caused relatively little direct attention to be paid to curriculum during the planning process: Department heads in the first school, for example, indicated that curriculum revisions began *before* "Focus" and simply went along parallel to it. Curriculum work was stimulated by the dean rather than by central administration. Documentary evidence substantiated this claim. The nine chairs interviewed in the second school—some from prestigious departments, others from relatively weaker ones—indicated that they saw "Focus" as a resource reallocation process; they barely mentioned curriculum reform as a part of the process or its results. One department head felt that curriculum would be addressed only in a back-door way: If additional slots were available, faculty would argue about what fields ought to be covered and from what perspective. Most felt that, before making any changes in their programs, they would wait for money and further evidence that changes would be rewarded.

The third school was almost recommended for closing. A mission definition (imposed by central administration) involved extensive changes in structure and program. But curriculum reform is a lagging consequence of these radical changes, not a major independent thrust; for example, the elimination of degree-granting programs requires the elimination of courses, as well as more cooperation with departments in other colleges that receive students after two years and so on.

Only one department chair was interviewed in the fourth school, and his attitude toward "Focus" as a stimulus for anything of value was rather negative.

In conclusion, according to department chairs, "Focus" provided at best a convenient label to paste on curriculum revision activities that were already in motion; in most cases, it has not been associated with curriculum changes in the core liberal arts and science departments. This supports Cohen and March's (1974) contention that, in multiversities, the influence of central administration is indirect and often barely acknowledged by the participants. Although curriculum reform may be initiated from the top, the real responsibility for it lies within the colleges and departments. Many organizational features within these departments will affect whether undergraduate educational improvement moves center stage or stays in the wings.

The Role of the Dean. At the University of Minnesota, deans could theoretically have used "Focus" as a vehicle for getting faculty to consider significant curricular and/or instructional reforms, but they were not always able to do so. A proposition based on reviewing the "Focus" process provides a possible explanation:

> *Proposition 4:* Deans of larger or more prestigious colleges are likely to have more influence with the central administration, since they control more resources; however, their influence among the faculty is inversely related to the size and prestige of the college.

Baldridge, Curtis, Ecker, and Riley (1978) have demonstrated that the role of the dean in the modern university is a very ambiguous one. Deans serve at the pleasure of the president but are not perceived to have the authority to tell departments what to do in matters of curriculum. Instead, influence must occur through persuasion. The ability to persuade faculty to become involved in schoolwide curriculum change depends on the existence of trust and respect between the dean and department chairs, since the latter are the main link between the college administration and the faculty. Creating a climate for influence requires interpersonal interaction (Riecken and Homons, 1954). If the reform activity requires cooperation between departments, this must occur in groups that are small enough to engender the necessary discussion.

Interviews with chairs from the University of Minnesota's two largest colleges indicated that they were much less involved in developing collegewide plans as a response to "Focus" than chairs in the smaller colleges, and they attended fewer meetings where they could compare the curriculum work being done in their own department with that of others. Furthermore, they did not necessarily perceive the dean as being particularly central to their department's own future regarding curriculum or other resources. In contrast, all of the department chairs in smaller colleges attended more meetings and expressed satisfaction not only with their involvement in the planning process but also with the use of "Focus" and of collegewide planning as a stimulus to department planning.

No matter what the influence of the dean, however, he or she is only a catalyst. As Conrad (1978) has shown, in academia there is hardly ever *one* leader in the change process, which usually produces a number of competing interest groups. Rather, the role of the leader, whether that person is the dean or department chair, is more that of a "lead mediator."

Department Cultures

The discussion thus far implies strong political and conflict components to the curriculum change process (Conrad, 1978; Lindquist, 1974). There is also a significant cultural component:

Proposition 5: In most universities, department influence over how individual professors allocate their time and energy can be rather profound (Louis, Blumenthal, Gluck, and Stoto, 1989). This mutual influence, however, rarely extends to curriculum or instruction.

There is often little collective work on curriculum. Rather, courses "belong" to a professor who exercises exclusive control over their content. Thus, in the extreme, hiring decisions determine the curriculum. Furthermore, existing values in most universities devalue work on undergraduate education. One social science faculty member may have spoken for many when he pointed out that to spend four years developing and managing a new submajor in the department while receiving lower than average raises because he had written fewer grant proposals than his peers sent a clear message. The individual in question *was* a productive publisher, and whether his statement is true is irrelevant; it reflects the belief system that conditions behavior.

Some departments are different, however. They hold values that do not celebrate autonomy for professors but that recognize collective responsibility for the undergraduate educational program. According to Kanter (1984), department cultures that promote an interest in collective (as opposed to individual) innovation:

- Provide incentives for collaborative work. For example, two professors collaborating on course development might both receive full "credit" for teaching the course.
- Don't pigeonhole people, but give them a broad territory in which to work. For example, most professors would agree that it is not necessary to be a scholarly expert in a field in order to teach undergraduate courses—particularly if these courses are approached in a new or unconventional way. The best teachers may design better courses than the specialists.
- Provide public praise and feedback and create a climate of pride in the department for both research *and* teaching. Emphasis on gathering data about the department's success with students (which is notably difficult for individual faculty to determine) would be particularly helpful.
- Provide rewards for involvement in curriculum work. Summer grants and course releases for active curriculum development can be very helpful. Recognition of outstanding teachers may help to

promote a sense that work with undergraduates is collectively valued.

These cultures can survive in research-intensive as well as less research-oriented settings. As Kerr (1964) points out, some multiversities have managed to maintain a strong emphasis on teaching and program quality while holding down spots in the top ten for decades. We can change department cultures, but it takes a long time and tangible institutional support from deans or central administration. Unfortunately, few department chairs are well versed in the art of political and cultural management. One suggestion for improving the curriculum change process, in addition to appointing chairs who value it, is to provide them with appropriate training in these skills.

Models for Change Management and Survival

A variety of models may apply to planning and implementing educational change. The model that the change manager should choose will depend on a variety of factors, including: the level of agreement about the nature of the problem and desirable solutions; the complexity and difficulty of the problems; and the energy available for change.

Managerial Planning Models. Where there is consensus on the need for change, the perceived problems are relatively straightforward, and conflict over possible solutions is low, the change planner can turn toward standard planning models that appear in management textbooks. Allison (1971) characterized these as "bounded rationality" models that emphasize a designated sequence of activities: diagnosis of a problem, information search, design of a plan for change, implementation, and evaluation. This chapter, however, suggests that universities rarely demonstrate these optimal characteristics.

More recently, higher education has paid attention to strategic planning, which is differentiated from standard planning by its explicit emphasis on altering mission and programs to reflect actual and projected changes in the university's environment (Clugston, 1987). Strategic planning also contrasts with standard planning in its consistent involvement of the top administrators of the organization. Although these features may promote many significant changes and a general recommitment to broad common goals, managerial planning models are unlikely to have a direct impact on major curriculum shifts in undergraduate education for all of the systemic reasons already discussed.

Incremental Planning Models. The most common alternative to the managerial models is variously referred to as "the science of muddling through" by Lindblom (1959) and the "garbage can model" (March and Olsen, 1986). The incremental planning approach is based on the idea that decisions in complicated, weak-culture organizations in turbulent settings have a quasi-random character. Planning is therefore symbolic more than it is an actual tool for improving performance. Advocates of this model—which, according to March and Olsen (1976), is particularly applicable to higher education—suggest that we should embrace this process rather than try to reform it (Brunsson, 1985). The assumption is that, in most circumstances, accumulated unplanned decisions to change made by competent and well-intentioned people will result in a natural, beneficial evolution of practice. Organizations that promote incremental decision making are also believed to be more inventive and adaptable. But abandoning a centralized planning process does not mean that administrators need sit back. Cohen and March (1974) derive a number of somewhat Machiavellian rules for influencing change in these contexts from their study of college presidents.

On the other hand, incremental decisions may not add up to enough when it comes to curriculum. In fact, curriculum planning in most major universities over the past twenty years has essentially followed this model, and we are clearly displeased with the results.

Evolutionary Planning Models. In the past few years, increasing attention has been paid to a synthesis of the incremental and managerial models. Pava (1986) and Louis and Miles (forthcoming) suggest a different set of images for managing change. Managerial planning suggests a constant striving for convergence among members of the organization, and incremental planning accepts the value of persistent divergence. An evolutionary planning model, on the other hand, emphasizes alternating convergence and divergence over a long period. The art of change management is knowing when to bring people together to develop some consensus on values and mission (as in strategic planning) and when to encourage diverse, localized experimentation. Over time, the organization evolves in a semiplanned, semiexperimental way. At the same time, administrators are responsible for slowly helping institutional members to develop a new consensus and values to support the new directions of the institution. As Pava (1986) puts it, "incremental change with pervasive systemwide implications [is] achieved by coupling the reinterpretation of values with grassroots change projects. . . . [It] reframes the status quo and eventually alters it indirectly. . . . This avoids threatening cautious and reluctant interests, while preserving the leeway needed to accommodate unanticipated developments" (p. 619).

The University's Management of Curriculum Change

The main issues facing multiversities that wish to create real reform in undergraduate programs are similar to those suggested by the Pava quotation. It is necessary to learn to operate within loosely organized, political settings but also to promote a movement toward consensus on a new role for undergraduate education within the institution. Making a major shift in values (such as moving from lack of concern with undergraduate education to an incorporation of it into the departmental and college value system) requires a number of interrelated design and management processes.

Apply Administrative Pressures for Change. Research in fields as diverse as business, anthropology, and economic development suggests an enduring principle of change: Top administrators must use their positions to create a sense of urgency and excitement (Miles and Louis, 1987). In large organizations, this sense of urgency must be reinforced at all levels. Administrative pressure is particularly crucial to promote difficult changes that require altering basic values and reward systems. The University of Minnesota's "Focus" process did provide a sustained commitment to change from the top for the duration of Keller's tenure as academic vice-president and president.

Find a Theme. Unlike traditional planning processes, an evolutionary planning model emphasizes neither broad missions nor specific objectives but a theme that promotes an image of what the college or department wants to become (Vaill, 1982). It is not just a slogan or a title for a project or activity. Instead, its imagery can be a rallying point for discussions of action. "Focus" attempted to provide this; however, it did not offer a real image of what might occur in the revisions to undergraduate programs. Individual deans needed to make the theme more specific for their colleges if they were to promote a clear image for curriculum change.

The role of change leaders in a political environment may be, as Conrad (1978) claims, that of "lead mediator." This chapter has asserted that changing undergraduate education in the university requires attention to the necessary cultural shifts as well. Thus, college leaders must also focus on ways of achieving an initial consensus on themes. In a university setting, this should occur broadly (that is, reflecting a genuine sense of the possible and desirable), but it need not always occur during a formal procedure to sense needs and concerns. Frequent informal interactions are more likely to promote attraction and agreement than opinion polls.

Start with People Who Have the Energy and Interest. Building loose coalitions of people who are stimulated by the theme is a critical initial activity. Guerrilla warfare is a better analogy for evolutionary change than the traditional military maneuver: It relies (at least initially) on small groups of volunteers, and it avoids a formal "top-down" process in the beginning (see Chapter Three). In addition, while small incentives are helpful, using significant resources to generate initial interest may simply encourage uncommitted entrepreneurship on the part of faculty or departments who like to be involved in anything that appears to have money and power behind it. New programs that begin on an entrepreneurial basis are less likely to persist than those accompanied by fewer resources (Louis, Rosenblum, and Molitor, 1982).

Promote "Action First." Managerial planning models assume that planning comes before action. But, in a politicized and fragmented environment, we should not assume that a plan will grab the imagination of the unconverted. This makes formal planning processes frustrating for planners and participants alike. However, an effective demonstration of activity that produces results with modest effort may change disbelievers into believers—and it also serves to energize and motivate those who are participating. This is particularly useful where contemplated changes lack precedents that connect a specific program to desired results. Arriving at a good undergraduate curriculum in a given university must be a matter of tinkering and learning through doing.

Action—as long as it is reasonably consistent with the theme—should be encouraged wherever there is interest. In evolutionary planning, "rolling enrollment" of interested people is often observed. People must be free to join and participate whenever they are ready, and the definition of who is on board and who is not must be made as loose as possible.

Provide Opportunities for Reflection and Celebration. An "action first" assumption is consistent with the incremental paradigm for planning and change. The evolutionary planning model requires time to reflect on the degree to which action is moving the department or college closer to its image. Action can take place in small groups or at the individual level, but reflection requires broader participation if it is to include and perhaps even co-opt the nonbelievers. Renewing and enlarging commitment to a new set of values are the goals, and the vehicles must be chosen carefully so they are not "just another meeting." Reflection may result in revising action—or even in revising the theme.

This last point is critical: Unlike a mission (enduring objectives) or goals (specific, short-term objectives), a theme is flexible and can be altered to fit the emerging common conception of what the college or department is about.

Allow for Buffering and Coping with Problems. This chapter has de-emphasized the technical side of the change—what *should* undergraduate education consist of. But the good change manager in higher education must understand that, over the long process in which a major institution shifts to a new direction, the technical core of the change will be at risk.

A common finding in qualitative studies of organizational change is that new programs are vulnerable to "normal crises." Normal crises do not occur on a regular basis; when they happen at a critical point in the development or implementation of a new program, they can result in its instant demise. These unanticipated problems represent indirect but more powerful threats to change than direct attacks or resistance. Normal crises include personnel changes, budget rescissions, strikes, the formation of new, powerful coalitions against the change—and, in the case of the University of Minnesota, the unanticipated departure of the president. Effective leadership, especially at the department and college level where networks are most dense, requires alertness to these possible events and the development of a commitment among both those with formal authority and those change leaders who emerge from the faculty to be vigilant in "coping."

Thus, in a large university, curriculum reform on an institutional level is difficult. Instead, change is likely to happen at the college level or below, where informal and formal networks of influence through departments and individual faculty dominate. In general, administrators will have less effect on curriculum reform than will broad social and professional trends. What administrators can do best is to provide "windows of opportunity" and support for change. For example, the presidency may be used as pulpit from which to argue for reform and to indicate support.

Implications

Thus, there is no manual or blueprint for change that administrators can turn to; no set of guidelines will always apply to all institutions. Rather, we need to develop an understanding of alternative approaches to designing and managing change in higher education and of when these alternatives represent reasonable choices.

If curriculum change is desired, it must be at the center of attention. Institutional change requires informal as well as formal networks of interpersonal influence through which reports of attitudinal and behavioral change can diffuse. This will not happen naturally in large, fragmented political institutions like multiversities. If institutional change, as opposed to pockets of individual attitudinal change or scattered program revisions, is desired, then college and department administrators in key communication positions should be encouraged to become "lead mediators" and change agents.

Above all, we must not struggle too fiercely against the basic characteristics of the university. No single institution or administration can alter the broad systemic characteristics noted at the beginning of this chapter. Instead, we should use evolutionary planning models to improve the odds that change will occur over time.

References

Allison, G. *The Essence of Decision.* Boston: Little, Brown, 1971.
Baldridge, J. V., Curtis, D. V., Ecker, G., and Riley, G. L. *Policy Making and Effective Leadership: A National Study of Academic Management.* San Francisco: Jossey-Bass, 1978.

Brubacher, J., and Rudy, W. *Higher Education in Transition.* (3rd ed.) New York: Harper & Row, 1976.

Brunsson, N. *Irrationality as a Basis for Organizational Action and Change.* New York: Wiley, 1985.

Clugston, R. *Strategic Adaptation in an Organized Anarchy: Priority Setting and Resource Allocation in the Liberal Arts College of a Public Research University.* Unpublished doctoral dissertation, University of Minnesota, 1987.

Cohen, M., and March, J. *Leadership and Ambiguity.* Berkeley, Calif.: Carnegie Commission on Higher Education, 1974.

Conrad, C. "A Grounded Theory of Academic Change." *Sociology of Education,* 1978, *51,* 101-112.

Kanter, R. *The Change Masters.* New York: Simon & Schuster, 1984.

Keller, K. H. *A Commitment to Focus: Report of Interim President Kenneth H. Keller to the Board of Regents.* Minneapolis: University of Minnesota, February 8, 1985.

Kerr, C. *The Uses of the University.* Cambridge, Mass.: Harvard University Press, 1964.

Lindblom, C. "The Science of 'Muddling Through.' " *Public Administration Review,* 1959, *19,* 79-88.

Lindquist, J. "Political Linkage: The Academic Innovation Process." *Journal of Higher Education.* 1974, *45,* 323-343.

Louis, K. S., Blumenthal, D., Gluck, M. E., and Stoto, M. A., "Entrepreneurs in Academe: An Exploration of Behaviors Among Life Scientists." *Administrative Science Quarterly,* 1989, *34* (1).

Louis, K., and Miles, M. *Getting There: Managing Change in Urban High Schools.* New York: Teachers College Press, in press.

Louis, K., Rosenblum, S. and Molitor, J. *Strategies for Knowledge Use and School Improvement.* Washington, D.C.: National Institute of Education, 1982.

Manns, C. L., and March, J. G. "Financial Adversity, Internal Competition, and Curricular Change in a University." *Administrative Science Quarterly,* 1978, *23,* 541-552.

March, J., and Olsen, J. *Ambiguity and Choice.* Oslo, Norway: Universitetsforlaget, 1976.

March, J., and Olsen, J. "Garbage Can Models of Decision Making in Organizations." In J. March and R. Wissinger-Babylon (eds.), *Ambiguity and Command.* Marshfield, Mass.: Pitman, 1986.

Miles, M., and Louis, K. "Research on Institutionalization: A Reflective Review." In M. Miles, M. Eckholm, and R. Vandenberghe (eds.), *Lasting School Improvement.* Leuven, Belgium: Acco Press, 1987.

Pava, C. "New Strategies of Systems Change: Reclaiming Nonsynoptic Planning Methods." *Human Relations,* 1986, *39,* 615-633.

Peters, T., and Waterman, R. *In Search of Excellence: Lessons from America's Best-Run Companies.* New York: Harper & Row, 1982.

Pfeffer, J., and Moore, W. "Power in University Budgeting: A Replication and Extension." *Administrative Science Quarterly,* 1980, *25,* 398-418.

Pfeffer, J., and Salancik, G. "Organizational Decision Making as a Political Process: The Case of a University Budget." *Administrative Science Quarterly,* 1982, *19,* 135-151.

Riecken, H., and Homons, G. "Psychological Aspects of Social Structure." In G. Lindzey (ed.), *Handbook of Social Psychology.* Vol. 2. Reading, Mass.: Addison-Wesley, 1954.

Snow, C., and Hrebiniek, L. "Strategy, Distinctive Competence, and Organizational Performance." *Administrative Science Quarterly,* 1980, *25,* 315-334.

Taylor, B. *Antioch: A and B.* Cambridge, Mass.: Institute for Educational Leadership, Harvard University Graduate School of Education, 1987.
Tichy, N. "Problem Cycles in Organizations and the Management of Change." In J. R. Kimberly, R. H. Miles, and Associates. *The Organizational Life Cycle: Issues in the Creation, Transformation, and Decline of Organizations.* San Francisco: Jossey-Bass, 1980.
Trow, M. "Continuity and Adaptability in Higher Education." *Educational Researcher,* 1988, *17,* 13-22.
University of Minnesota. *A Strategy for Focus: Guidelines to the College.* Minneapolis: University of Minnesota, November 3, 1986.
Vaill, P. "The Purposing of High Performing Organizations." *Organizational Dynamics,* Autumn 1982, pp. 23-39.
Weick, K. "Educational Organizations as Loosely Coupled Systems." *Administrative Science Quarterly,* 1976, *21,* 1-19.

Karen Seashore Louis is associate professor in the Department of Educational Policy and Administration, University of Minnesota.

Research serves multiple purposes in institutional renewal. Successful tactics for change require clear definition of research objectives and campuswide support.

Research and Assessment: Tools for Change

Warren W. Willingham

Educational change is a broad topic with a vast literature. My purpose is not to survey the problems and the possibilities of this complex subject but to address a narrow question: How can research and assessment encourage beneficial change? Delbecq and Mills (1985) recently argued that innovation is dependent on the interaction among three variables: the motivation to innovate, the obstacles against innovation, and the number of resources available. Clearly, research and assessment consume rather than create resources. So the question becomes: How can research and assessment enhance the motivation to innovate and diminish the obstacles?

I will pursue three approaches to this question. First, it is useful to consider how research and assessment are related to the driving forces that actually cause change. It is also useful to examine the received wisdom about the role and utility of research and assessment. Finally, I will discuss some specific research and assessment tactics and how they might be useful.

In the course of these comments, I will often speak as if research and assessment are much the same. They are not, of course, even though the one often involves the other. Assessment is better at monitoring and describing, while research is better at exploring and evaluating. For our purposes, however, it is convenient to speak generally of research and assessment simply as research—a technically oriented tactic to be contrasted with action programs or administrative decisions that are based on experience, informed judgment, or consensus.

Major Sources of Educational Change

The role of research and assessment seems especially relevant to planning changes in institutional policies and issues. By institutional, I mean the educational system generally, as well as individual colleges and universities. I will discuss eight major wellsprings of change. They are interrelated and they overlap, though each often involves somewhat different motivations and obstacles and a different role for research.

Reform Movements. One wellspring is the reform movement, which has a long tradition in this country. Such movements arise from within the academy, but they often involve some rejection of conventional forms, such as the usual program, the traditional content, or the accepted practice. Reform movements propose solutions—sometimes radical departures—in the hope of bringing about dramatic improvements. Some movements live passionately but briefly. Some continue to perk along, even with the disinterest of the educational establishment. Most leave some mark.

Reform movements normally reflect an ideology. For that reason, they usually depend on and are much associated with strong leadership. Reforms have come in different stripes and shapes. Some, like the "new math," sprang from a discipline. Others, like nontraditional study, laid siege to the entire educational process (Keeton and Associates, 1976). Curriculum revisions within the professions and in general education account for some of the more prominent reform movements. Reform also encompasses a multitude of organizational experiments—that is, changes in the form of institutions and the ways in which they offer their programs (Heiss, 1973; Dressel, 1971).

Research often takes a muted role in reform movements. Reformers lean toward activism. They tend to use research only when it serves their purposes. One purpose may be fact finding, but ideological reform seems more typically based on a persuasive rationale or a value argument. Program evaluation sometimes comes into play, but it is usually not the tough scientific variety. More often it is a demonstration project—that is, a concrete verification that the new program works well or at least that it provides a benign alternative to the usual way of doing things.

Structural Modifications. The organizational experiments of reformers suggest this second major source of educational change. Two historic changes in the structure of higher education stand out. The last half of the nineteenth century saw the development of the land-grant universities. The last half of the twentieth century has been particularly associated with the development of community colleges. The former revolutionized higher education by incorporating research and service as basic institutional functions. The latter provided universal higher education in local communities within a coordinated state system. These massive structural modifications brought with them a dramatic broadening of the mission of higher education and untold changes in curriculum and services.

It seems safe to say that research and assessment had little to do with inspiring these changes. On the other hand, public universities and community colleges have made extensive use of state and local needs assessments in order to shape programs and services. Such structural changes dealt with domestic needs. When the Soviets sent up Sputnik in the 1950s, it posed a different type of problem. This external threat offered the specter of an educational system that had lost its lead. That shock wave incited major federal spending and intensive new efforts at all educational levels—especially in science and language education. Thus, we come to a third mechanism of educational change:

Funded Programs. Federally funded programs came into their own in the 1960s—the days of the Great Society. Huge amounts of money were directed to the improvement of many social institutions, education in particular. In this mechanism of educational change, research and assessment—along with development—play a critical catalytic role. These are the means by which whoever is in charge intends to shake things up. Money is the carrot. For shaking, it works extremely well. For improving, the record is spotty. Nevertheless, funding remains the method of choice for getting something to happen. Private foundations know that; so do state legislatures.

Popular Mandate. Social needs also give rise to a fourth source of educational change—a mechanism we might call the popular mandate. Thirty years after Sputnik, we have a counterpart that provides an example of the popular mandate. In 1983 the National Commission on Excellence in Education warned, "The educational foundations of our society are being eroded by a rising tide of mediocrity that threatens our very future as a nation and a people" (p. 5). The authors bolstered their rhetoric with facts. For example, the report stressed the consistently poor performance of American students in comparative national studies. In several such studies, our young people placed last among industrial nations. Thus, research and assessment often play a central role in the formation of a popular mandate. Laying bare disturbing facts can quickly focus attention and motivate action.

There have been other reports and much debate as to causes and blame for the current state of education. Notice, however, that the preferred remedies are quite different from those of thirty years past. Rather than fund new research, new development, and new programs, the inclination now is to try to raise educational standards by mandating new requirements, such as new certification tests for teachers, new leaving examinations for high school seniors, and new course requirements for college matriculants (Breland, 1985; Goertz and Johnson, 1985; Goertz, 1986). Assessment has come heavily into play. Whether the medicine produces a cure is another question, and the side effects of the medicine are the source of another debate. The point is that a strong public consensus can change educational practices surprisingly quickly.

Legal Mandates. These recent responses to public demands suggest this fifth source of educational change. I refer particularly to legislation and court decisions that protect the interests and rights of groups within the broader society. A prominent legislative example is the GI Bill, a seminal act in the democratization of higher education. The interplay between legislation and court decisions can have profound effects on institutions. Title IX (1972) comes immediately to mind. The Supreme Court's decision in *Grove City College* v. *Bell* (1984) was widely perceived to limit severely the applicability of the act's provisions to higher institutions, but then came reinstating legislation, aptly named the Civil Rights Restoration Act (1987).

The role of research in relation to such legal mandates is usually secondary. In one narrow sense, however, research is sometimes critical. Quantitative analysis, often quite technical, has become commonplace in judicial determinations as to whether groups are adequately represented, whether tests are valid, and whether selection is fair. But these are not issues that bear heavily on the topic at hand.

Economic Survival. I shift now to a different issue, a problem more specific to the institution. Nothing focuses the mind like a threat to survival or continued good health. It provokes new attitudes and new questions about goals, effectiveness, and cost-benefit relationships. It can inspire propositions for change that would otherwise hardly be contemplated. With an external threat to institutional health, the problem is not motivation for change but obstacles. Research is one tool sometimes used here—the most applied type of research imaginable.

The commonly perceived threat to many institutions in recent years has been the downturn in the number of traditional college-age youth. Years ago the certain prediction of this downturn incited feverish activity among many institutions who saw themselves under the gun. In order to avoid financially unacceptable declines in enrollment, many colleges undertook aggressive marketing efforts, sometimes based on sophisticated information systems and mathematical analyses (Litten, Sullivan, and Brodigan, 1983). Institutions have recruited new types of students to their campus—notably more women, minorities, and older adults—and intensified their efforts to develop new programs to meet student interests. Such changes have taken place selectively, but in aggregate they appear to be substantial. They will likely increase over the next five to ten years.

Technological Advance. Another contemporary problem for many institutions is keeping up with technology. Certainly, technological advance is another major source of educational change. Some time ago, computers changed the way institutions do business. Increasingly, they are changing the way students learn and the way instructors teach (Bunderson, Inouye, and Olsen, 1988). For obvious reasons, this is a research-intensive avenue to educational change. Computers not only facilitate research to a remarkable degree; they also inspire a different type of scholarship and problem solving and a different attitude about what constitutes sufficient information.

Institutional Renewal. It might appear that the sources of educational change I have described are heavily reactive: responses to a mandate, a social problem, a threat, or to the happy availability of funds. That appearance is partly accurate, due to my having saved until last the source of change that is most important and largely dependent on the initiative of faculty and staff. I refer to the year-in year-out process of institutional renewal—not sweeping changes that are ideological or controversial, but the difficult business of maintaining an effective institution with programs and services of high quality.

All institutions face the constant tasks of doing a better job, adapting to new problems, and capitalizing on new opportunities. These tasks have to be worked at all the time. Robert Hutchins (1968) was known for urging innovation as a way of life for institutions: "The whole business about a university and about education can be summed up in a question: Has the institution vitality? Is anything going on? Is there anything exciting about it? This is the only test of a good university" (p. 21).

There is, of course, a great deal of disagreement as to whether too little or too much is going on in higher education. Hefferlin (1969) describes one perspective as follows: "Critics point to rampant academic faddism, bandwagon fashion, uncritical innovation, and helter-skelter efforts at modernity in following the peddlers of untested nostrums" (p. 5). Clark (1962) expressed in similar hyperbole, what may be the more prevalent view: "Many schools and colleges are unable to make any change until confronted by crisis—near bankruptcy or an exodus of staff or an explosive split among key personnel" (p. 194).

Hefferlin (1969) summarized good reasons for institutional inertia. Most organizations are inherently passive, they attract members who agree with their activities, and they tend toward ritualism. He adds that academic institutions have additional barriers to innovation. They are horizontally and vertically fragmented, their reputation is not based on innovation, and they are staffed with independent professionals who are often skeptical about the notion of efficiency in academic life. Without arguing the accuracy or the ramifications of those assertions, let me move on to the obvious question: How can research and assessment be better used to foster and support institutional renewal? Part of the answer, I believe, lies in the role that educational research has played in the past and in how it is perceived. What is the received wisdom?

The Role of Research and Assessment

One can distinguish three forms of received wisdom on the role of research and assessment in encouraging useful educational change: technical wisdom, humanistic wisdom, and conventional wisdom. Each of these labels sounds vaguely suspect, and that is no accident. There is something seriously lacking in all three, though each has some merit.

Technical Wisdom. Those who embrace the technical wisdom are unabashedly enthusiastic about research, assessment, and technology as useful tactics in solving educational problems. This is the scientific approach. It symbolizes receptivity to new ideas as well as hardheaded objectivity. Most important, it offers some possibility of separating fact from fiction and distinguishing useful new approaches from superstition and dogma. But there are serious flaws and shortcomings to the technical view of problem solving.

We should not assume that this technical wisdom is the exclusive property of people bathed in technical smarts. For example, most of us have been socialized to assume that the certified research finding is necessarily consequential. A finding is certified in various ways: by powerful statistics, arcane experimental design, and significance at the $p = .05$ level—preferably $p = .01$. This attitude often leads to premature enthusiasm for ideas that have little practical significance. Furthermore, there is the related tendency to focus undue attention on research method, rather than on the validity and utility of findings and on whether they will generalize to another situation.

These problems are related to the refreshing but naive view that a compelling research result is sufficient to alter an educational practice. In fact, such decisions get made by people who have the authority to make them and the responsibility to deal with the aftershocks and side effects. There are always other facts to consider, other values to weigh, other restraints and complications in the real world.

What is the conclusion? Certainly technical tools are important, but careful analysis of the practical meaning of technically derived findings is essential. Uncritical acceptance of dubious facts is as bad as arguing that all important facts are unknowable, except in some intuitive way.

Humanistic Wisdom. The stereotype goes as follows: If some aspect of human behavior is truly important, it cannot be measured.

Furthermore, two conditions or individuals are never alike. So-called objective research and assessment of the human condition are pseudoscientific because they standardize the very individuality they attempt to understand. Thus, these tactics of educational problem solving are, at best, trivial and, at worst, dangerous.

In this brand of received wisdom, the central point concerns the superiority of judgment over so-called objectivity and quantification. The problem is that subjective judgments must always face the music of objective verification. To argue otherwise is to say, for example, that experts cannot judge one piece of work to be more competently executed than another or that the opinions of experts are not accountable to other opinions or facts.

When subjective judgment is persistently out of line with facts, one ultimate dodge is to assert, "This one is different. This time I'm sure." In his classic monograph, *Clinical Versus Statistical Prediction,* Paul Meehl (1954) answers that point as follows:

> "Why should we care whether you think this one is different or whether you are surer?" Again, there is only one rational reply to such a question. We have now to study the success frequency of the clinician's guesses when he asserts that he feels this way.... Always, we might as well face it, the shadow of the statistician hovers in the background; *always* the actuary will have the final word (p. 138).

Probably so. Antiquantification sentiments are often grossly exaggerated. Nonetheless, we still have the basic worry. In the rush to objectivity, it is glaringly easy to overlook critical factors that we are not measuring and to disregard the fact that people and situations vary.

Conventional Wisdom. It is generally understood that conventional wisdom is, by convention, incorrect. There are, however, two forms of conventional wisdom: the traditional, which we insiders know to be incorrect, and the current, which we have not yet so recognized—or perhaps which we have not had sufficient opportunity to subvert. I particularly associate the traditional wisdom about educational research with the Great Society programs of the 1960s.

Once an important educational problem is identified, the traditional wisdom is applied in five steps: (1) Provide money. Inadequate resources are the reason it is difficult to improve educational practice. (2) Unleash the researchers on this problem. They will come up with many good new ideas. (3) Give the researchers a couple of years to tell us which innovations work. It will probably take that long to do the job right. (4) Give the research reports to the people out in the schools and colleges. Seeing a good thing, they will implement it. (5) Observe the improvements—just like in the research project.

It is easy to see now that these are very often unrealistic assumptions. Good ideas are hard to come by and even harder to make practical and implement. Ideas that actually work in practice are often sabotaged by inadequate follow-through. Thus, the acceptance of this traditional role for educational research—to stimulate experiments and sort out the ones that worked—diminished markedly in the 1970s.

The current wisdom about research and assessment takes a different tack. Now the emphasis is on assessment—particularly assessment as a means of ensuring accountability and maintaining standards. This is a notable difference. Traditionally, research was used in the hope of discerning and expanding effective educational programs. Now, the focus is on evaluation of results of ongoing programs, and the strategy is to offer money for demonstrably good outcomes.

It sounds as if it makes good sense. Why is this wisdom likely to become conventional? A built-in danger is the "quick fix." Both innovation and accountability are administratively impatient. The impulse is to get on with it. Good research and good assessment, on the other hand, are reflective, labor intensive, and time intensive. They grind along, putting out a report a few months or years hence. Meanwhile, the busy administrator has been distracted by another crisis and may have trouble remembering why the project was started in the first place.

Savvy administrators know about all of this. They do not normally make the mistake of providing enough time to solve the problem. If expediency is the rule, there are two likely results, both bad. One is to go through the motions and leave the problem undisturbed. Another possibility is that the results of narrowly based, standardized assessments are overused in making judgments about people or programs.

That is not what is intended, of course. Even William Bennett (1986), the most noted advocate of the assessment hard line, urged the use of "many different methods—standardized tests, interviews, questionnaires, reviews of students' written work over four years, studies of alumni and dropouts." The influential report, *Involvement in Learning* (Study Group on the Conditions of Excellence in American Higher Education, 1984), stressed the following good practices in assessing outcomes of education:

- Assessing knowledge and skills developed in academic as well as cocurricular programs
- Assessing what is appropriate to the competencies addressed and to the educational objectives of the institution
- Involving faculty in all aspects of assessment
- Providing feedback for the improvement of learning.

The question, of course, is: Will anyone listen to this good advice? Already in this same report, we see some signs of self-destructing wisdom. I refer to the recommendation on page 55 that institutions measure

the same competencies at graduation as at entry. Without pointed qualification, such advice surely encourages simplistic applications of the value-added approach to educational accountability. I count these among the more serious drawbacks of the pretest to posttest design:
- The very limited applicability of the notion of freshman-to-senior-year gain
- The egregious technical errors it provokes
- The very narrow definition of higher education that is unwittingly fostered
- The erosion of standards that is implied by valuing gain, irrespective of actual competence and knowledge.

In this discussion of the role of research and assessment in educational change, I have alluded to a number of problems: outcomes that are often ambiguous, multiple criteria for evaluating those outcomes, the typical state of partial knowledge, the difficulty of transporting technical results into the real world, the problem of deciding what to measure, and the competing values in doing so. All of this is to say that, with research and assessment, you can expect a lot of disappointment, to say nothing of the occasional shot in the foot—that is, learning something you did not really want to know.

Having scaled the heights of skepticism, what do I have good to assert? Principally, that the alternative—not using whatever technical help you can get—is a lot worse. Intelligently used, research and assessment yield enormous benefits in clarifying questions, forcing issues, rationalizing debate, vitalizing the educational process, justifying new departures—even getting closer to the truth. I move now to the ways in which these benefits come about.

Tactical Uses of Research and Assessment

It is important to make a distinction between longer- and shorter-term educational change. A primary function of higher education institutions—universities, in particular—is to help improve the educational process by developing those disciplines that are especially concerned with the effectiveness of instruction and student support services. Indeed, effective learning and pedagogy are concerns of all disciplines. Certainly the research and scholarship that lead to long-term improvement of teaching should be a continuing priority. Such work is critical in building theory, developing methods, and exploring uncharted domains. The following discussion, however, is directed to the tactical use of research and assessment in support of more immediate opportunities for change—especially what I have called "institutional renewal." I will comment briefly on six such tactics. These are, to a considerable degree, complementary rather than alternative tactics; in combination they can foster an overall assessment ethic and an openness to change.

Maintaining a Factual Foundation. A continuing challenge for all institutions is effective adaptation to changing circumstances. Without good information, administrators who try to bring off a successful adaptation face an uphill battle. Indeed, one of the great frustrations of administrative life is the lack of appropriate information. Maintaining an adequate factual foundation for planning and policy discussion is one of the fundamental ways in which research and assessment support useful educational change. Such a factual foundation consists of critical indicators of institutional functioning and institutional environment. These indicators include student characteristics and attitudes, many forms of academic bookkeeping, and such contextual matters as demographics and financial factors.

These facts serve several purposes. They alert the institution to troublesome trends or differences across units or groups of students; in other words, they can motivate changes where needed. They also provide factual backup when objections to change are raised; thus, they help administrators deal with obstacles. And they help give an appropriate shape to whatever changes are proposed.

Institutions appear to have improved greatly in maintaining a good factual foundation, though progress is uneven. Three steps seem particularly important. One is careful selection of the critical indicators. When their number gets beyond all bounds of reasonableness and usefulness, they become an "information system." A second important step is to develop an economical procedure for assembling such information so that it is not only accurate but also comparable across years and units. A third and dreadfully difficult step is to disseminate the information so that it is accessible to and actually useful to those who need it.

Mandating Summative Assessment. Nothing seems to provoke discussion of institutional change quite like serious assessment of learning outcomes. Just the proposition that such assessment might take place often raises questions about the adequacy of current educational practices. Grades don't do it. Grades are nonspecific as to what students have actually learned. Also grades slide about in curious ways, influenced by such factors as subject matter, course level, composition of the class, and instructor philosophy.

By "mandating summative assessment" I mean putting to the faculty the job of deciding how educational outcomes should be assessed. There have been several useful reports on this topic in the past few years (Ewell, 1984; Rossman and El-Khawas, 1987; Adelman, 1986). Outcomes assessment is certainly best approached in an open-ended manner, but several framing questions are likely to prove useful:

1. What constitutes adequate mastery of a baccalaureate degree program? What forms of acquired competence represent the unique contributions of higher education, as qualitatively different from those

competencies that students might be expected to gain naturally in non-college endeavors?

2. Among such competencies, which generic skills or knowledge apply to all departments or programs? Which apply to specific courses of study? Which represent effective individualization of higher learning?

3. What levels of such competencies represent adequate achievement in an undergraduate program? What levels deserve special recognition?

4. What methods of assessment are appropriate to the competencies involved and will yield results so that it is apparent from the assessment process itself whether appropriate levels of accomplishment have been attained?

5. In what ways can it be assured that all important learning outcomes related to institutional and program objectives are appropriately considered, whether the learning occurs in or out of class?

Supporting Formative Assessment. A third way of motivating educational change is to foster and provide funding for formative assessment of student achievement. By "formative assessment" I mean a systematic effort to determine whether students are successfully acquiring particular knowledge and skills that are critical to mastering their field. Mastery should be seen as the accomplishment of personal learning goals that go beyond minimum competence. Assessment of higher forms of mastery is likely to require complex procedures, such as oral and written presentations, problem solving, and demonstrations of the ability to perform tasks that apply academic competence to real-life situations.

Such assessment has to do with tracking educational progress, not with determining who should be admitted or who should graduate. Evidence that students are making steady gains indicates that the system is working, that the effort is paying off. When students are not making progress, it becomes clear that something is wrong. Such assessment can also contribute to institutional accountability, but I stress here the usefulness of formative assessment in revealing ways in which the system is not working well—that is, its usefulness in motivating educational change.

Clarifying Policy Issues. Research and assessment can also play a key role in another tactic for educational change. It is a tactic somewhat related to fact finding but goes far beyond. I refer to the deliberate use of research and assessment to probe issues that would not otherwise be raised, to identify desirable changes, to assemble supporting evidence. This is a demanding analytic function; it is heavily policy oriented and often demands attention from the highest level of an institution's administration.

There are at least two variations. One is the use of research and assessment to launch and support a serious program of institutional renewal. Facts are systematically marshaled through special studies, surveys, and so on in order to examine the need and explore the options for redirection. Recent studies inspired by the University of Minnesota's "A Commitment to Focus" (Keller, 1985) provide a good example (see *Plan for Focus,* 1987).

Another variety is the watchdog or monitoring model. Many aspects of institutional functioning move along from year to year, seldom subjected to careful scrutiny; such aspects include grading practices, regulations governing academic standing, and views of faculty and staff on institutional priorities. We need to ask more tough questions. The use of probing institutional research is a way of doing that. It seems to me that institutional research needs to be reinvigorated; it has lost some of its zip.

Legitimizing Sound Programs. A fifth tactical use of research and assessment in educational change is to prove and legitimize. This is akin to the time-honored pilot study or full-dress evaluation, but all efforts to evaluate educational changes are not undertaken with scientific detachment. Often, the object of such efforts is to legitimize an apparently sound educational program that is largely unused due to skepticism as to the program's respectability or its practical effectiveness. So the ostensible purpose of the experimental project may be to test and improve the idea, but the main agenda may be simply to demonstrate its reasonableness, to show that it actually works. The real interest is to remove obstacles.

Research projects to prove and legitimize are well suited to certain types of change: the promotion of alternative procedures, the introduction of new technology, or the erection of new structural models for delivering education. The literature of educational reform provides examples, such as the demonstration from the 1930s that students could succeed in college even if they did not all follow the same traditional curriculum in secondary school (Aiken, 1942). A more recent example is the Cooperative Assessment for Experiential Learning's Project's demonstration that more rigorous assessment of learning outcomes can materially improve the credibility of nontraditional education (Willingham, 1977).

Encouraging Research Involvement. A sixth tactic is to involve faculty and staff systematically in institutional research. There are two reasons why this tactic is effective. One concerns obstacles to change, the other motivation. For institutions—particularly large ones—to deal successfully with complex problems, collaboration is essential. Units have to coordinate; diverse expertise must be brought to bear. Perhaps most important, one has to involve the parties ultimately affected to ensure that proven ideas actually get carried out.

There is a more subtle and, I suspect, more important benefit to involving people in institutional research: to capture attention and commitment. Deep involvement changes the way people think about consequential issues. Getting people engaged with a problem is a Trojan horse, a nose under the tent. Extensive involvement of faculty and staff was a hallmark of pioneer institutional research at the University of Minnesota (Eckert and Keller, 1954).

Let me conclude with two comments. First, effective research and assessment tactics do not necessarily pop up by themselves, like dandelions on a spring lawn. They require some fertilizer: money plus institutional commitment at a high level. Second, research can promote useful change, but good ideas do not come easily. When an exciting new research project comes to mind, sobering experience leads me to recommend this four-point test:

1. Will my findings have a significant bearing on any consequential policy or practice?

2. Assuming I get perfect results, just as predicted, will anyone care?

3. Have I involved the people without whose cooperation actual use of the findings could not possibly succeed?

4. Have I anticipated and dealt with alternative interpretations and with claims that the results are invalid or inapplicable?

Assuming one has passed this four-point test and all signs are favorable, the road ahead becomes a personality test. Before investing too much in a good idea, some consult further with friendly skeptics. Others charge blindly ahead. It is this latter group who often create the excitement in education—and sometimes the trouble.

References

Adelman, C. (ed.). *Assessment in American Higher Education.* Washington, D.C.: Office of Educational Research and Improvement, 1986.
Aiken, W. *The Story of the Eight-Year Study.* New York: Harper & Row, 1942.
Bennett, W. Testimony Before the Senate Committee on Labor and Human Resources' Subcommittee on Education, Arts, and the Humanities, January 28, 1986.
Breland, H. *An Examination of State University and College Admission Policies.* ETS Research Report, no. 85-3. Princeton, N.J.: Educational Testing Service, 1985.
Bunderson, C., Inouye, D., and Olsen, J. "The Four Generations of Computerized Educational Measurement." In R. L. Linn (ed.), *Educational Measurement.* (3rd ed.) New York: Macmillan, 1988.
Civil Rights Restoration Act, 20 U.S.C. sections 1687-1688 (1987).
Clark, B. *Educating the Expert Society.* San Francisco: Chandler, 1962.
Delbecq, A., and Mills, P. "Managerial Practices That Enhance Innovation." *Organizational Dynamics,* 1985, *14* (1), 24-34.
Dressel, P. (ed.). *The New Colleges: Toward an Appraisal.* Iowa City: American College Testing Program and American Association of Higher Education, 1971.
Eckert, R., and Keller, R. *A University Looks at Its Program.* Minneapolis: University of Minnesota Press, 1954.

Ewell, P. *The Self-Regarding Institution: Information for Excellence.* Boulder, Colo.: National Center for Higher Education Management Systems, 1984.

Goertz, M. *State Educational Standards: A Fifty-State Survey.* ETS Research Report, no. 86-2. Princeton, N.J.: Educational Testing Service, 1986.

Goertz, M., and Johnson, L. *State Policies for Admission to Higher Education.* College Board report, no. 85-1; ETS Research Report, no. 85-26. New York: College Entrance Examination Board, 1985.

Grove City College v. Bell, 456 U.S. 555 (1984).

Hefferlin, J. *Dynamics of Academic Reform.* San Francisco: Jossey-Bass, 1969.

Heiss, A. *An Inventory of Academic Innovation and Reform.* Berkeley: Carnegie Commission on Higher Education, 1973.

Hutchins, R. "Trees Grew in Brooklyn." *The Center Magazine,* 1968, *1* (7), 21.

Keeton, M. T., and Associates. *Experiential Learning: Rationale, Characteristics, and Assessment.* San Francisco: Jossey-Bass, 1976.

Keller, K. *A Commitment to Focus: Report of Interim President Kenneth H. Keller to the Board of Regents.* Minneapolis: University of Minnesota, 1985.

Litten, L., Sullivan, D., and Brodigan, D. *Applying Market Research in College Admissions.* New York: College Entrance Examination Board, 1983.

Meehl, P. *Clinical Versus Statistical Prediction.* Minneapolis: University of Minnesota Press, 1954.

National Commission on Excellence in Education. *A Nation at Risk: The Imperative for Educational Reform—A Report to the Nation and the Secretary of Education, United States Department of Education.* Washington, D.C.: National Commission on Excellence in Education, 1983.

Plan for Focus: Commitment to Focus Advisory Task Force on Planning. Charles E. Campbell, Chair. Minneapolis: University of Minnesota, 1987.

Rossman, J., and El-Khawas, E. *Thinking About Assessment: Perspectives for Presidents and Chief Academic Officers.* Washington, D.C.: American Council on Higher Education and the American Association for Higher Education, 1987.

Study Group on the Conditions of Excellence in American Higher Education. *Involvement in Learning.* Washington, D.C.: National Institute of Education, 1984.

Title IX of the Education Amendments of 1972, 20 U.S.C. sections 1681 et seq.

Willingham. W. W. *Principles of Good Practice in Assessing Experiential Learning.* Princeton, N.J.: Educational Testing Service, 1977.

Warren W. Willingham is Distinguished Research Scientist and assistant vice-president for program research at the Educational Testing Service, Princeton, New Jersey.

Large institutions, often criticized for not delivering high-quality undergraduate education, can use the faculty's applied research activities to improve the student experience.

Pathways to Success: Transforming Obstacles into Opportunities

Joan B. Garfield, Darwin D. Hendel

Large institutions are not often known for the quality of the undergraduate experience on campus. In Astin's (1977) longitudinal study of college students, for students who attended large universities, there was low student involvement on campus, little interaction with faculty, and lower likelihood of student achievement in the arts, leadership activities, and athletics. Several of the eight tension points (such as separation between academic and social life on campus and divided loyalties between teaching and research) in undergraduate education noted by Boyer (1986) are especially problematic in large institutions. Issues of quality of the undergraduate experience are critical because of the large numbers of students who attend such colleges and universities across the country.

Students attending these multiversities usually enroll in large lecture courses, often taught by graduate assistants, for their first classes. Students may find it difficult to establish contact with faculty, teaching assistants, and even other students. Due to large enrollments, students may spend hours registering, buying books, and getting frustrated with the administrative red tape required for many routine procedures. Students often feel that no one really cares about them or knows they are

C. H. Pazandak (ed.). *Improving Undergraduate Education in Large Universities.*
New Directions for Higher Education, no. 66. San Francisco: Jossey-Bass, Summer 1989.

there. They exacerbate the problem by sitting in the back of large classes, not seeking out instructors during office hours, and initiating few personal interactions.

Large institutions known as research universities pose additional problems for undergraduates. Geiger (1985) found that undergraduate colleges at research universities usually contain slightly less than half of the student enrollment but consume considerably less of the institution's budgetary resources. Geiger described the stereotype that faculty tend to neglect undergraduates in order to pursue their own research. Edgerton (1985) has suggested that faculty members' immersion in their disciplines leads to a "blind side" regarding pedagogy. Faculty need to be encouraged to use their research interests to improve the undergraduate experience and to communicate to colleagues on campus the potential applications of activities under way elsewhere in their institutions.

Despite the research that exists on college teaching and learning (McKeachie, Pintrich, Lin, and Smith, 1986), little of it is being translated into practice. Even at large research institutions, which bring in large sums of external money to fund research, little activity is focused on improving undergraduate education. Sullivan (1985) and Donald (1985) have suggested that what is lacking is specific, practical research that involves faculty in projects related directly to improving the student experience. Long advocated by Cross (1988) as the type of educational research with the most impact, research by individual faculty members is often not shared among colleagues in large universities.

The University of Minnesota is not alone among large institutions in a resurgence of interest in improving the undergraduate experience and in using research as one basis for change in undergraduate education. Similar efforts at the University of California, the University of Pittsburgh, and the University of Arizona attest to the increased interest in using faculty expertise to facilitate such change. The chapters in this sourcebook point to efforts at diverse institutions that have the potential for significant change.

In spite of cynicism about the role and importance of undergraduate education, most large institutions could describe numerous efforts at improvement. Among the activities at the University of Minnesota are the following: the Alliance for Undergraduate Education, a group of twelve national institutions working collaboratively on projects to improve undergraduate education; the Bush Collaboration Project, a regional, externally funded faculty development project; the Educational Development Program, an institutional program to fund faculty projects to improve the student experience; and Undergraduate Research Opportunities, a program to fund undergraduates to work with faculty on research projects. These and other activities demonstrate how large institutions can turn obstacles to improvement into opportunities for change.

In addition to ongoing institutional efforts to improve undergraduate education, numerous faculty are involved in research and development activities that have the potential for application across their institutions. In planning for a program on this subject, we found more examples of successful projects than could be featured in a single conference session. Those described in the following pages are but a few of them. They illustrate how academic support structures and institutional planning efforts can encourage development and experimentation that lead to improvements in the student experience. These showcased activities were of great interest to individuals attending the conference. We think of them as "pathways to success" and hope that they inspire others to adapt them for use at similar institutions.

Each research-based project originated with one or more individuals' dissatisfaction with an aspect of undergraduate education. Some projects were funded internally; others began with external funding. The following descriptions include a statement about why the project was needed, an outline of the nature of the project, and an overview of what was learned and what changes have resulted.

Curriculum Development Efforts

Although the University of Minnesota as a whole is still wrestling with important, emerging questions about its liberal education curriculum, selected individuals, departments, and colleges have made significant progress in revising undergraduate curricula at the university. The following two examples demonstrate how curriculum revision projects can benefit from faculty members' research interests.

Teaching Ethics in Dentistry. Recent technological developments in the health sciences have resulted in increased interest in the role of ethics. Studies of dental students' abilities to deal with ethical issues and their attitudes about ethics have confirmed the need to rethink the role of formal instruction in ethics.

Research by a faculty member in the School of Dentistry (Bebeau, 1985) provided the foundation for a curriculum project designed to help students deal with ethical problems in dentistry. The project applied a theoretical approach to the study of ethical development in dental education.

Over a four-year period, students spend approximately fifty hours resolving ethical problems. Activities in year one include: pretesting on the Defining Issues Test and Dental Ethical Sensitivity Test, feedback on assessment results, and discussion of additional preclinical ethical issues. Year two continues the discussion of preclinical ethical problems. Year three emphasizes peer review of ethical cases. Year four includes individual sessions with practitioners, lectures on professional roles, advanced discussion of ethical problems, and posttesting.

Studies of the impact of the curriculum revision have demonstrated the effectiveness of the structured learning activities in enhancing the clinical performance of dental students. The model used in dentistry has been adapted and incorporated into curriculum revisions in other health services programs in other colleges in the institution.

Project Sunrise. Declining student interest in majors in agriculture, concerns from employers about the qualifications of recent baccalaureate graduates, and the rapidly changing technologies in food production all suggested that the curriculum in agriculture needed significant attention.

This project, sponsored by the Kellogg Foundation, began with a review of the undergraduate curriculum in the College of Agriculture. Interviews with faculty members, employers, and recent graduates were used to determine what is necessary to prepare graduates for careers in agricultural disciplines. Attention was placed on both content and process aspects of the curriculum, with a goal of integrating ability and skill outcomes (such as problem solving and teamwork) into discipline-based courses.

Among the approaches used to accomplish this goal have been minigrants to individual faculty, seminars and retreats for faculty on integrating skills development into their courses, and applied research on some of the ability areas.

Applied research and evaluation have played an important role in the development of Project Sunrise. Surveys of faculty and advisers about courses, focus-group interviews with prospective employers, and participant evaluation forms for sponsored activities have been used to formulate and revise project activities. The next step will be to work with faculty to assess the outcomes (such as the development of critical thinking) that have resulted from students' participation in the revised curriculum (Pechtel, 1988).

Classroom Research

Another type of activity consists of applied research conducted by individual faculty within the context of courses they teach. The following examples summarize two efforts by individual faculty members to use pedagogical research activities to improve classroom instruction.

Pair Problem-Solving Strategies in Developmental Mathematics. Students underprepared in mathematics in large universities enroll in remedial mathematics courses that are often taught by disinterested graduate assistants or faculty with little preparation in teaching remedial math. Students in such classes often have low self-concepts as math learners, a past history of failure in math, and high levels of test anxiety. All of these factors result in high attrition rates in developmental mathematics courses.

An instructional method (Koch, 1988) in which students work in pairs to solve problems and become more aware of their thinking and reasoning skills has been used to improve instruction in developmental math. Class time is divided into three types of sessions: pair problem-solving activities, small-group discussions, and large-group discussions of mathematics problems and related concepts.

Preliminary results suggest decreased levels of negative self-concepts and anxiety about math and increased retention rates in remedial classes. The approach is being expanded to include sections of elementary algebra classes as well as basic mathematics. Research on how this intervention affects student performance and attitudes is being continued and expanded so that student persistence and success in higher-level mathematics courses may be determined.

Using Computers with Learning-Disabled Students. Learning-disabled students have low completion rates in basic college writing classes, in part because they need more time to complete assignments. As increasing numbers of learning-disabled students enroll in college programs, innovative instructional strategies need to be developed to help students complete freshman composition requirements and additional writing requirements in higher-level courses.

A federally funded grant was obtained to design and implement a microcomputer-based writing course (Collins, Engen-Wedin, Margolis, and Price, 1987). Groups of diagnosed learning-disabled students and of regular students both received instruction in using computers and had access to computers and word-processing software throughout a two-quarter freshman writing course.

At the end of the second term, both groups of students produced writing samples that were scored by objective nonaffiliated raters. The study indicated that microcomputers improved performance in writing and developed more positive attitudes toward writing among learning-disabled college students. This project suggests that the microcomputer serves as an effective "equalizer" for learning-disabled college students.

As a result of this project, the college has changed the way it uses computers with students. Microcomputers are now used routinely with all students enrolled in basic writing classes in the General College. The project also has been adapted by other similar institutions for use with their learning-disabled students.

Student Services Projects

Colleges of all types and sizes are faced with meeting the needs of a changing generation of entering college students. The following two examples describe efforts to improve student services for particular groups of students typically found in large institutions.

Group Advising with High-Risk Minority Students. Underprepared minority students in large colleges and universities require special attention if they are to develop appropriate academic behaviors and succeed in their first year in college. Even when special support services (such as tutors, counselors, and special sections of introductory courses) are offered, students often do not use them.

New minority students were recruited to participate in weekly groups of about six students each during the first term (ten weeks) of college. Various intervention models from the counseling psychology literature guided the sessions on the premise that the academic success of these students is directly related to three factors: study skills, personal development, and behavioral management.

Both quantitative measures of self-concept, study skills, and academic performance and qualitative data gathered from interviews (Rivas, 1988) were used to compare students in the group intervention with a control group of students who participated in regular sessions with individual advisers. Results indicated that the group intervention increased students' confidence about succeeding in college, made them more knowledgeable about the skills they needed to succeed, and helped them achieve grades comparable to other liberal arts students.

The effort is being replicated in other units at the university and also has stimulated undergraduate advisers to rethink their strategy for dealing with underprepared, high-risk minority students.

Comprehensive Student Services for Disadvantaged Students. Disadvantaged first-year college students often feel that they do not belong in college, that they have little family support for their attending college, and that they have no place to call home on a large campus. Especially in large institutions, students may be less knowledgeable about registration procedures and may enroll in courses that require writing and mathematics skills that they lack.

Students who meet specified eligibility criteria are offered an integrated system of student services. These services include regular meetings with counselors or advisers, reserved places in sections of courses, tutorial assistance, social functions at which students can become acquainted with each other, and a campus home for them to "check in" with people who know them and are concerned about their progress.

Annual evaluations of students' academic success and of their retention and transfer rates (Schmitz and Calvin, 1988) indicate the effectiveness of coordinating student services for disadvantaged first-year college students. The success has resulted in changes in selected student services for all entering students in the college. The two components of early monitoring of student progress and reserved places in introductory classes are especially likely to be useful in large institutions.

University-Wide Projects to Assess Outcomes

Another type of successful activity includes projects to assess important aspects of undergraduate education. These activities reflect institutional concerns and look at the impact of college on students.

Sophomore Assessment Project. Liberal education curricula in large institutions often resemble a smorgasbord of courses with little continuity. It is unclear who is responsible for lower-division outcomes, since the predominant emphasis in large institutions is on instruction within the major.

This research project (Hendel, 1988) focused on assessing learning outcomes of students' first two years at the university, examining the extent of agreement among instruments purported to measure the same constructs and relating those outcomes to students' course selection patterns. Four instruments (the Academic Profile, the College Outcome Measures Project, the Defining Issues Test, and the Sophomore Assessment Project questionnaire) were administered in the spring of 1988 to a sample of students who had completed more than half of the course work required for graduation. Resulting data have been provided to the Senate Committee on Educational Policy (SCEP) and to other committees on campus to help them rethink the institution's liberal education requirements and consider a more widespread procedure for assessing learning outcomes of undergraduate education.

Survey of Baccalaureate Degree Candidates. Especially in large institutions, it is difficult for programs and departments to have a clear sense of how educational experiences are viewed by students. Lack of feedback from consumers results in static programs that may have serious weaknesses in the minds of students. Although individual colleges, programs, and departments had conducted periodic surveys of soon-to-graduate students, the institution had no campuswide procedure that reflected students' perceptions of their college experiences.

As a result of recommendations contained in several recent university task force reports, the offices of the vice-presidents for academic affairs and for student development worked together to develop a survey instrument and procedure to collect information from baccalaureate degree candidates. The four-page survey (Matross, 1988) contains questions about course work and instructors in both general education and the major, advising and related student services, the campus environment, and perceived benefits and gains from attending the university. Students expecting to graduate spring quarter 1988 were asked to complete the survey as part of the degree clearance process.

Responses from 2,199 students (77 percent of those who applied to graduate) were used to prepare a campus report, collegiate reports, and departmental reports that were distributed widely across campus. Comments about survey content are being used to revise the survey and to develop a final version of the instrument to be used on an annual basis for graduating seniors.

Perspectives

Although numerous other problems with the student experience remain unaddressed, these and additional efforts clearly demonstrate the feasibility of significant improvements in undergraduate education at large institutions. They demonstrate how faculty members' research interests, coupled with opportunities for external funding, can serve as stimuli for improving the curriculum and related student services. The eight projects described here have inspired others in the institution to implement similar activities. Conference participants indicated that the research-in-practice sessions were outstanding examples that held promise for adaptation. The fact that many individuals were previously unaware of the initiatives points to the particular need for structured sharing activities in large institutions.

When asked what next steps were needed, conference participants noted the need for more encouragement at all levels of efforts to improve the quality of the student experience. Large institutions need to redirect money to support these types of projects and to change the reward system so that interested faculty are encouraged to participate. Isolation among those interested in improving the student experience is a problem in large institutions. Our next task is to establish networks of interested faculty who can collaborate on further research-based projects, and we need to identify additional ways of encouraging faculty to focus their research expertise on improving undergraduate education.

References

Astin, A. W. *Four Critical Years: Effects of College on Beliefs, Attitudes, and Knowledge.* San Francisco: Jossey-Bass, 1977.

Bebeau, M. "Teaching Ethics in Dentistry." *Journal of Dental Education,* 1985, *49* (4), 236-243.

Boyer, E. L. *College: The Undergraduate Experience in America.* New York: Carnegie Foundation for the Advancement of Teaching, 1986.

Collins, T., Engen-Wedin, N., Margolis, W., and Price, L. "Learning-Disabled Writers and Word Processing: Performance and Attitude Gains." *Research and Teaching in Developmental Education,* 1987, *4,* 13-21.

Cross, K. P. "In Search of Zippers." *AAHE Bulletin,* 1988, *40* (10), 3-7.

Donald, J. G. "Directions for Future Research and Its Applications." In J. G. Donald and A. M. Sullivan (eds.), *Using Research to Improve Teaching.* New Directions for Teaching and Learning, no. 23. San Francisco: Jossey-Bass, 1985.

Edgerton, R. "It All Begins in the Classroom: An Interview with K. Patricia Cross." *AAHE Bulletin,* 1985, *38* (1), 3-7.

Geiger, R. "Research Universities: Their Role in Undergraduate Education." In Study Group on the Condition of Excellence in American Higher Education, *Contexts for Learning: The Major Sectors of American Higher Education.* Washington, D.C.: National Institute of Education, 1985.

Hendel, D. D. "Assessing Outcomes of Lower-Division Instruction." Paper presented at the Conference on Improving Undergraduate Education Through Research and Practice, Minneapolis, Minnesota, May 6-7, 1988.

Koch, L. "The Effectiveness of Pair Problem Solving in a Developmental College Mathematics Class." Paper presented at the Conference on Improving Undergraduate Education Through Research and Practice, Minneapolis, Minnesota, May 6-7, 1988.

McKeachie, W. J., Pintrich, P. R., Lin, Y., and Smith, D.A.F. *Teaching and Learning in the College Classroom: A Review of the Literature.* Ann Arbor: National Center for Research to Improve Postsecondary Teaching and Learning, University of Michigan, 1986.

Matross, R. "Using Surveys of Graduates to Improve Undergraduate Education." Paper presented at the Conference on Improving Undergraduate Education Through Research and Practice, Minneapolis, Minnesota, May 6-7, 1988.

Pechtel, B. "The Role of Applied Research in Curriculum Revision in the College of Agriculture." Paper presented at the Conference on Improving Undergraduate Education Through Research and Practice, Minneapolis, Minnesota, May 6-7, 1988.

Rivas, M. "An Exploratory Study of a Group Intervention for Underprepared Minority University Students." Unpublished doctoral dissertation, University of Minnesota, 1988.

Schmitz, C., and Calvin, C. "The Impact of a Proactive, Comprehensive Student Services Program on Academic Success of Disadvantaged Students." Paper presented at the Conference on Improving Undergraduate Education Through Research and Practice, Minneapolis, Minnesota, May 6-7, 1988.

Sullivan, A. M. "The Role of Two Types of Research on the Evaluation and Improvement of University Teaching." In J. G. Donald and A. M. Sullivan (eds.), *Using Research to Improve Teaching.* New Directions for Teaching and Learning, no. 23. San Francisco: Jossey-Bass, 1985.

Joan B. Garfield is an associate professor in the Division of Science, Business, and Mathematics in the General College, University of Minnesota.

Darwin D. Hendel is a research associate in the office of the vice-president for academic affairs, University of Minnesota.

Evaluation, especially when based on a stakeholder-centered model of inquiry, can positively influence institutional change.

Achieving Excellence: How Will We Know?

Clifton F. Conrad, David J. Eagan

How will we know if the curricular changes and innovations we have painstakingly designed, nurtured, and introduced are having any significant effect? Finding out is not a simple task, nor are the results likely to be unambiguous, but such evaluation is of the utmost importance to those committed to bringing about successful change.

Program changes and innovations, whether driven by a private vision or by external mandates, often take on a life of their own once introduced. Partly because curriculum is largely self-propelled and partly because our attention is constantly demanded elsewhere, universities have a tendency to omit the crucial and probably most difficult step in program improvement: assessing impact and consequences. Instead, the assumption is typically made that change, because it is intended to improve, is invariably a good thing. While this may be true to a point, the assumption prevents our finding out exactly what has improved and by how much. It is important that this sourcebook on curricular change include a close look at the process of evaluation as a mechanism for helping institutions to know if excellence has been achieved. This chapter focuses on facilitating evaluation in large institutions, although examples will also be drawn from other settings. We will use the terms *assessment* and *evaluation* interchangeably. Each is sufficiently ambiguous in meaning to defy precise application, but, in general, we consider assessment, which has lately been tied somewhat narrowly to student outcomes measures, to be a subset of evaluation.

The Challenge of Evaluation

The process of planning for and evaluating change invariably challenges the resourcefulness and stamina of academic institutions buffeted by local, state, and national demands for accountability and curricular improvement. Public institutions in particular have come under intense scrutiny and pressure, and their programs, finances, and missions have been questioned as seldom before. Demands for change and improvement have driven a national scramble to upgrade mission statements and establish new programs, curricula, and, recently, comprehensive assessment initiatives at the program, institutional, and state levels.

Unfortunately, our institutional propensity for launching innovations is only infrequently accompanied by a commitment to assessing the efficacy of what we have done. The University of Minnesota, for example, has a long history of supporting curricular innovations and new programs, but those involved admit that many of those projects have not been accompanied by adequate evaluation. This shortcoming is understandable, given the reward structure and often conflicting expectations of the modern university, but it is clearly not ideal. Innovations and change efforts must be wedded to an evaluation strategy for purposes of determining if a particular project is achieving what it set out to do and of identifying inadvertent outcomes.

Assessment and evaluation are especially nettlesome at large, complex institutions where departmental independence, diffused leadership, and unclear channels of accountability may undermine such monitoring efforts (Dinham, 1988a). Moreover, the pursuit of "excellence" carries so many meanings in today's multiversity that the consensus required in order to make constructive use of evaluation results may be possible only at the least complex levels.

We can best understand the numerous issues embedded in the evaluation of change and innovation by taking into account multiple perspectives on them. Thus, this chapter brings together pertinent literature on evaluation, assessment, program review, and program quality. Relevant examples of evaluation approaches from selected universities are included to ground the discussion in institutional experience.

Choices for Action and Reflection

There are numerous accounts in the literature concerning assessment and evaluation practices in higher education, ranging from statewide assessment plans (Banta and Fisher, 1984), to institutional assessment plans, to evaluations at the departmental and program level (Conrad and Wilson, 1985). While these project descriptions often contain ideas worth considering in designing evaluations, we are rightly cautioned by Ewell (1985) that "each project is distinctive, and none should prompt direct imitation" (p. 4). Rather, he suggests that we glean an understanding of the choices made in project design and, if possible, the consequences that follow from these choices. In that vein, we propose that a useful approach to evaluation is to examine key decision arenas that deserve attention in any assessment plan.

At large institutions, the strategy for assessing and evaluating change must match the scope of the changes attempted, the institutional context, the people affected, and the financial stake in its success. The larger the project, the greater the challenge in identifying and keeping track of factors that are beyond control. The "realities of the evaluation world," as Patton (1980) calls them, work against the evaluator "who strives to obtain the best possible design and the most useful answers within the real world of politics, people, and methodological prejudice" (p. 18). Obstacles multiply as the scope of a project grows, as those of us in large universities know only too well. One result is that less assessment activity is found at large institutions than at smaller ones (Ory and Parker, 1989).

Notwithstanding the inevitable caveats encountered, a review of the relevant literature presents planners and administrators with a variety of important considerations in the design of an evaluation strategy. In each of these decision arenas, the relative merits of competing philosophies and approaches must be judged. The choices, for example, between qualitative and quantitative measurement and between formative and summative evaluation hold opportunities as well as pitfalls in assessing institutional change.

In this chapter, we discuss six decision arenas where choices made among alternatives are likely to have a significant impact on the evaluation effort. These categories are not exhaustive, nor are they as discrete and clear-cut as the discussion may make them appear. They represent some of the major areas of concern in the literature and professional discourse regarding evaluation, assessment, and program quality. There is a much wider literature that should be explored before final decisions are made; this discussion is intended only to introduce the categories of choice. We bring this "paradigm of choices" (Patton, 1980, p. 20) into consideration both to sharpen awareness of critical issues in evaluation and to lend a measure of concreteness to the discussion through the use of case examples.

Purposes. We assume here that curricular change has been initiated in order to improve existing conditions at an institution and that the findings of an evaluation will be used to further that improvement.

While it can be argued that ultimate uses must await evaluation results, it is nevertheless important to consider the likely uses beforehand in order to aim the study in a direction that can serve the targeted ends. At the same time, an openness to unanticipated uses that arise during or at the conclusion of the evaluation can further enhance improvement.

Building agreement on the purposes of evaluation is a critical preliminary step. The careful consideration of aims and purposes at the outset will expedite subsequent choices as well as guide the overall evaluation design. An evaluation of curricular change can be based on the view that change is iterative, requiring periodic monitoring and corrective input. Or it can focus primarily on the outcomes of the change effort, resulting in a need for summary judgment. These two broad purposes—formative and summative—are not mutually exclusive, but evaluation designers need to choose where to place the strategic emphasis.

Formative. Evaluations that are formative in emphasis (Scriven, 1967) are conducted on an ongoing basis to determine the effectiveness of a project during its implementation and to inform improvements. This approach is favored by those who desire continuous feedback on which to base ongoing adjustments in their implementation strategy. Assessment designed using a formative approach openly reflects a commitment to view evaluation as a kind of learning instrument that guides rather than criticizes. As such, it can serve the interests of those affected by curricular change as well as those responsible for ensuring its effectiveness.

Summative. Evaluating the effectiveness of program change at the end of an arbitrary period constitutes a summative approach (Scriven, 1967). In practice, this is more common than a formative approach and finds wide application in educational settings. Most kinds of student testing and student outcomes measurement address the end product of a course or curriculum, asking, "Did the changes work as intended?" Value-added and norm-referenced measures are typically used to address this question, and input from those being evaluated is often minimal. Decisions about continued funding or program continuance often hinge on the findings of summative judgments.

Involvement and Control. The responsibility for choices made in the design, implementation, and use of an evaluation typically rests with an individual (such as an outside evaluation expert) or group (usually members of the institution) assigned the necessary authority. The decisions that this person or group makes affect all aspects of the evaluation; the interplay of personalities, social and cultural dynamics, and politics needs to be taken into consideration throughout.

In addition to determining where control rests, evaluation designers need to establish the degree of involvement of interested individuals and groups, who can often exert considerable influence. The following alternatives illustrate a conceptual division between a broad-based and a more narrow administrative locus of control, although in decentralized institutions like many large universities the distinction is often blurred.

Broad-Based Control. The involvement of stakeholders—defined as any person or group with a direct interest in the outcomes of a change or innovation—has long been recognized as critical to an effective evaluation. Who is more fitting to judge the quality and worth of a program than those most directly involved? However, even minor curricular reform in large universities can affect substantial numbers of people, challenging planners to sample opinions accurately. Because of the inherent difficulties, an honest involvement of stakeholders requires serious effort.

Stakeholders can be incorporated into every step of the process, from the initial identification of purposes to adjustments made during implementation to the translation of findings into policy decisions. We distinguish, of course, between involvement and control, realizing that most of the consequential decisions regarding evaluation design will ultimately be made by those in control. The "responsive" evaluation model (Stake, 1975), which is discussed later, emphasizes this broad-based approach and supports the claim that stakeholder involvement maximizes ownership of both the evaluation and its results.

Administrative Control. The responsibility for virtually all curricular change in colleges and universities resides within an administrative hierarchy. Yet how this responsibility is delegated and the roles that administrators play are open to strategic variation: Strict top-down leadership is at one end of the continuum and dispersed control at the other. Within the context of administrative control, an evaluation can be designed to encourage either broad or narrow participation among the units that are directly affected.

Strong administrative leadership has been cited as a key factor influencing success in program implementation and evaluation (Conrad, 1978). The success of outcomes assessment initiatives under way in a number of states has been attributed to the singular commitment of a university president or other high-ranking individual (Provost's Steering Committee on Assessment, 1987). Administrative leaders can offer a vision of the potential accomplishments of program innovation and change and can have significant impact on involvement and long-term success.

Focus and Scope. Inevitable limits in resources and time make it advisable to restrict the scope of a project to those areas of greatest concern that can be dealt with fully. These constitute the "short list" of areas to be examined. A short list helps ensure that the evaluation will concentrate on areas where it can have the greatest effect.

Among the factors influencing project scope, institutional politics will probably play a significant role. Accordingly, assessing the political climate may be necessary before deciding what aspects of change to evaluate. At large universities in particular, there will often be political expedients—that is, larger payoffs—linked to certain areas targeted for evaluation. But, if such choices are made only for political reasons, they may result in what Edelman (1977) terms "words that succeed and policies that fail." Within the context of these concerns, the scope of an evaluation will range from broad to narrow.

Comprehensive. An evaluation of curriculum change can take a broad, comprehensive view, addressing a host of factors that affect the implementation and outcomes of change. As an example, the assessment plan at the University of Arizona places major emphasis on the total undergraduate experience, taking into account the initial capabilities of students, the academic curriculum and extracurriculum, elements of the institutional environment, and a broad range of student outcomes (Conrad, 1987). The newly established Center for Research on Undergraduate Education coordinates these efforts. At Arizona, where the aim of assessment is institutional improvement, a comprehensive approach is deemed essential in revealing overall context and ongoing change. Such large projects are characterized by greater complexity and ambiguity, but they also hold the potential for richer analysis.

Specific. An evaluation effort may be aimed specifically at measuring and judging the effectiveness of curricular change from as narrow a perspective as desired. The assessment program at the University of Arizona, in addition to its more global perspective, provides for specific evaluation efforts to respond to "current questions" that arise within the institution (Dinham, 1988b); shorter-term, focused attention is given to special problems and concerns. Evaluations designed to judge the effectiveness of specific programs or isolated curricular modifications may be less hampered by complexity of the sort found in comprehensive efforts, but their findings may also have more limited application.

Evaluation Models. Criteria, evidence, and judgment are the common threads uniting all evaluation efforts into a sort of kinship, however distant the relationship may appear. They are at the core of all evaluations, regardless of the rhetoric and packaging that can make different approaches appear to be polar opposites. This is not to imply that the methods chosen to pursue these threads make little difference. On the contrary, hundreds of research articles and books are devoted to the exploration of the many concerns and debates associated with the evaluation task. Although much of the earlier literature centered on explicating methodological approaches to evaluation, current practice and theory often explore evaluation from the context of utilization and decision making (Patton, 1978; Weiss, 1988; Shapiro, 1986).

Complex projects at large institutions may call for several concurrent evaluative strategies, involving the use of methodologies and orientations from two or more models. The selection of models needs to be based on their usefulness in addressing the project emphases generated from previous design choices (on purpose, scope, focus, and stakeholder involvement). The many overviews of evaluation models in the literature can provide a helpful orientation to the field and can aid in determining which approach is best suited for a particular institution (Gardner, 1977; Madaus, Scriven, and Stufflebeam, 1983; Conrad and Wilson, 1985; Shapiro, 1986). The following is a summary of four major evaluation models, based on the typology of Conrad and Wilson (1985).

Goal-Based Model. Variations on this model predominate in evaluation efforts in higher education and are grounded in the work of Tyler (1949). Evaluating the attainment of objectives is at the heart of the goal-based approach. Previously established program goals, objectives, and standards of performance are identified, program outcomes are measured, and a judgment is made based on the congruence or discrepancy between planned objectives and demonstrable outcomes (Gardner, 1977). While a goal-based approach is typically summative in intent, Provus (1971) has expanded the scope of the model to serve formative purposes as well by including analysis and interpretation of intended program processes in addition to outcomes.

Responsive Model. The responsive approach is organized broadly around "the concerns and issues of stakeholding audiences" (Guba and Lincoln, 1981, p. 23). Originally developed by Stake (1975), the responsive model stresses that evaluation efforts should not be driven narrowly by program goals but rather that an understanding of "unintended effects" (Scriven, 1973) and of stakeholder concerns is necessary for interpreting outcomes. The design of a responsive evaluation is an ongoing process, since each step is informed in part by previous activity (Guba and Lincoln, 1981).

Decision-Making Model. Some educators believe that the ultimate purpose of an evaluation effort is to inform administrative decisions. Thus, this model is organized around the decision-making process. The most widely known decision-making model is the Context, Input, Process, Product (CIPP) model (Stufflebeam and others, 1971), which holds that the different types of decisions inherent in the evaluative process require different kinds of evaluation activities. Four types have been identified: context evaluation, which assists decision makers in determining goals and objectives; input evaluation, which helps clarify alternative ways of achieving program goals and objectives; process evaluation, which provides feedback to decision makers; and product evaluation, which provides decision makers with information as to whether a program should be continued, modified, or terminated. While the CIPP approach has not been widely applied in higher education, the number of institutions initiating decision-oriented evaluation is increasing (Conrad and Wilson, 1985).

Connoisseurship Model. In many instances, evaluations are entrusted to persons whose expertise qualifies them to judge the relative merits of a program in all its complexity, subtlety, and nuance. Under the connoisseurship model (Eisner, 1976), the connoisseur alone guides the evaluation, balancing and comparing information gleaned through documents, interviews, and observation with a continuous, more intuitive awareness and sense of appreciation, which Eisner likens to the appreciation of art. The visits of accreditation review teams are based partly on this model; team members' extensive experience gives them a connoisseurship on which to base their judgments about program quality.

Evaluation Emphasis. An important arena of choice in evaluation concerns the emphasis on program versus that on product—in other words, whether to assess curricular change from the viewpoint of the program itself or from its outcomes. Each orientation provides different kinds of information about quality and effectiveness that can serve decisions from either a formative or summative perspective. Both emphases can be combined in an evaluation, multiplying the complexity of the task but providing a more complete analysis.

The "assessment movement" in higher education, with its expanding base of scholarly literature and growing institutional practice, illustrates how this difference in evaluation emphasis plays out in institutional settings (Ewell, 1987). While most institutions have focused their attention on the outcomes of the undergraduate experience, many have attempted to look as well at the learning environment and other conditions that may influence outcomes. The choosing and implementing of an assessment emphasis or "model" is no simple matter, however, as Ewell and Boyer (1988) imply in their examination of recent assessment experiences in five states (Colorado, Missouri, New Jersey, South Dakota, and Virginia).

Academic Program, Environment, and Student Characteristics. The quality and impact of the academic and institutional environment, which can have significant effects on student achievement, are troublesome to measure. Because of this difficulty and also because of mandates for assessments and evaluations that emphasize data on outcomes, little systematic effort has targeted this area.

The comprehensive assessment project at the University of Arizona, however, provides an instructive example. Through a variety of measurement strategies, the Arizona Plan (Conrad, 1987) seeks to identify and assess factors in three broad areas that influence student outcomes: student characteristics, including knowledge, attitudes, and intellectual skills; components of the undergraduate experience, specifically general education, the major, and the extracurriculum; and institutional environment, composed of climate, resources for learning, faculty, students, and curriculum. Examining these factors provides a context within which decision makers can interpret evaluation results.

Outcomes. In higher education, the prevailing emphasis in evaluation studies is on measuring student outcomes. Most efforts seek to assess educational proficiency or gain in student knowledge and skills, though some strive to document student growth in other areas as well. Alverno College is frequently cited for its commitment to a comprehensive student assessment strategy that is integrated fully with the curriculum and that measures such student abilities as problem solving, valuing, and taking environmental responsibility (Alverno College Faculty, 1985; Mentkowski and Loacker, 1985). Similarly, the "talent development" approach to achieving educational excellence (Astin, 1985; Jacobi, Astin, and Ayala, 1987) takes a holistic approach to measuring long-term student growth and development.

Most outcomes assessment approaches, however, place primary emphasis on testing and other quantifiable measures of student achievement. The value-added method, which assesses gain in knowledge and skills over time as measured using pretests and posttests, forms the core of the assessment program at Northeast Missouri State University (McClain and Krueger, 1985). At the University of Tennessee at Knoxville, a performance-based funding assessment effort uses value-added tests such as the American College Testing College Outcomes Measures Project (ACT COMP) to measure student achievement in both the major and general education (Banta, 1985). In many institutions, nationally normed tests such as the GRE and MCAT are also employed. In an instructive treatment of this topic, Jacobi, Astin, and Ayala (1987) address many of the limitations of outcomes measurement and urge the choosing of testing instruments that match the goals and values of an institution.

Methods of Measurement. Effective evaluation requires that measurements be as accurate and meaningful as possible. The literature in evaluation and related fields, especially in critical reviews and meta-analyses, contains extensive debate over methodology, much of it centered on problems of measurement. An ongoing quarrel focuses on the tendency in education, as in the social sciences overall, to value quantitative over qualitative techniques (Cook and Reichardt, 1979; Patton, 1980; Bednarz, 1985). The design of an evaluation needs to address the balance between these two techniques, weighing the relative merits of each.

Quantitative. Quantitative measurement is prevalent in evaluation and assessment in which data are based on test scores, survey statistics, Likert-type scales, and other numerically oriented measures. Such data are frequently viewed as the most scientific and, hence, the most valid and reliable kinds of information. In goal-based evaluations, for example, many of the criteria used to compare objectives with outcomes are grounded in some quantifiable measure of performance. An overarching concern must be that such quantitative data reflect reality as closely as possible.

Qualitative. Increased attention has been focused in recent years on naturalistic and qualitative approaches to evaluation (Lincoln and Guba, 1985). Interviews, open-ended survey questions, and participant observation are qualitative methods that can add the depth and meaning that is not easily captured through quantitative techniques. Moreover, case studies (Merriam, 1988) and ethnographic evaluation (Tierney, 1985) are qualitative approaches aimed at extracting ideographic and cultural meaning from educational settings.

Conclusion

The foregoing arenas for choice are perhaps best conceived as overlapping pieces of a larger picture, each existing in a dynamic balance with the others. Making choices among them is not necessarily an either/or matter but should be viewed as a process of balancing alternatives that seem most fitting for a given set of circumstances.

Historically, many of us in higher education have been more adroit at initiating change—or, rather, forging ahead with new ideas—than we have been at evaluating realistically and thoroughly the changes we have introduced. We are, first, creators and planners and, second, evaluators and formal critics. In higher education today, there is probably one evaluation committee for every dozen committees planning for change.

In many ways, implementing high-quality programs is a never-ending, Sisyphean task. Just when we think excellence is within reach, new priorities and circumstances often arise that refigure our institutional trajectory. Evaluation can take away some of the guesswork in implementing our ideas and can help guide us into more promising directions for future change and innovation. Furthermore, deliberate assessment and evaluation can reveal aspects of quality and areas of concern that were unanticipated in the original project design. Jacobi, Astin, and Ayala (1987), for example, describe several unanticipated effects of value-added assessment, such as increased student test anxiety, awareness of intellectual development, and better test-taking skills. From the perspective of these researchers, successful evaluation projects not only measure effectiveness but also produce an impact themselves. Similarly, we believe that carefully designed evaluation efforts can have a positive influence on overall institutional development, as well as on the specific change they originally set out to assess.

In closing, we urge that serious attention be directed to the evaluation of curricular change in order both to understand the consequences of that change and to recognize the significance of change to all relevant constituent groups. Such attention will lead, we hope, to a model of inquiry centered on the stakeholder (Conrad, 1989), which in turn will lead to a broader consensus about and commitment to what it takes to achieve excellence.

References

Alverno College Faculty. *Assessment at Alverno College.* Milwaukee, Wisc.: Alverno Productions, 1985.
Astin, A. W. *Achieving Educational Excellence: A Critical Assessment of Priorities and Practices in Higher Education.* San Francisco: Jossey-Bass, 1985.
Banta, T. W. "Use of Outcomes Information at the University of Tennessee at Knoxville." In P. T. Ewell (ed.), *Assessing Educational Outcomes.* New Directions for Institutional Research, no. 47. San Francisco: Jossey-Bass, 1985.
Banta, T. W., and Fisher, H. S. "Performance Funding: Tennessee's Experiment." In J. K. Folger (ed.), *Financial Incentives for Academic Quality.* New Directions for Higher Education, no. 48. San Francisco: Jossey-Bass, 1984.
Bednarz, D. "Quality and Quantity in Evaluation Research: A Divergent View." *Evaluation and Program Planning,* 1985, *8* (4), 289-306.
Conrad, C. F. "A Grounded Theory of Academic Change." *Sociology of Education,* 1978, *51* (2), 101-112.
Conrad, C. F. *Plan for Assessing Undergraduate Education at the University of Arizona.* Tucson: Task Force on Assessment of the Quality and Outcome of Undergraduate Education, University of Arizona, 1987.
Conrad, C. F. "Meditations on the Ideology of Inquiry in Higher Education: Exposition, Critique, and Conjecture." *Review of Higher Education,* 1989, *12* (3), 199-220.
Conrad, C. F., and Wilson, R. F. *Academic Program Reviews.* ASHE-ERIC Higher Education Report, no. 5. Washington, D.C.: Association for the Study of Higher Education, 1985.
Cook, T. D., and Reichardt, C. S. *Qualitative and Quantitative Methods in Evaluation Research.* Beverly Hills, Calif.: Sage, 1979.
Dinham, S. M. "Issues and Methodological Concerns for Undergraduate Assessment in Large Research Universities." Paper presented at the annual meeting of the Association for the Study of Higher Education, St. Louis, November 3-6, 1988a.
Dinham, S. M. *Summary of Assessment Activities at the University of Arizona.* Internal Report, no. 4. Tucson: Center for Research on Undergraduate Education, University of Arizona, 1988b.
Edelman, M. *Political Language: Words That Succeed and Policies That Fail.* Orlando, Fla.: Academic Press, 1977.
Eisner, E. W. "Educational Connoisseurship and Criticism: Their Form and Function in Educational Evaluation." *Journal of Aesthetic Education,* 1976, *10* (3-4), 135-150.
Ewell, P. T. (ed.). *Assessing Educational Outcomes.* New Directions for Institutional Research, no. 47. San Francisco: Jossey-Bass, 1985.
Ewell, P. T. "Assessment: Where Are We?" *Change,* 1987, *19* (1), 23-28.

Ewell, P. T., and Boyer, C. M. "Acting Out State-Mandated Assessment: Evidence from Five States." *Change,* 1988, *20* (4), 40–47.
Gardner, D. E. "Five Evaluation Frameworks: Implications for Decision Making in Higher Education." *Journal of Higher Education,* 1977, *48* (5), 571–593.
Guba, E. G., and Lincoln, Y. S. *Effective Evaluation: Improving the Usefulness of Evaluation Results Through Responsive and Naturalistic Approaches.* San Francisco: Jossey-Bass, 1981.
Jacobi, M., Astin, A. W., and Ayala, F., Jr. *College Student Outcomes Assessment.* ASHE-ERIC Higher Education Reports, no. 7. Washington, D.C.: Association for the Study of Higher Education, 1987.
Lincoln, Y. S., and Guba, E. G. *Naturalistic Inquiry.* Beverly Hills, Calif.: Sage, 1985.
McClain, C. J., and Krueger, D. W. "Using Outcomes Assessment: A Case Study in Institutional Change." In P. T. Ewell (ed.), *Assessing Educational Outcomes.* New Directions for Institutional Research, no. 47. San Francisco: Jossey-Bass, 1985.
Madaus, G. F., Scriven, M., and Stufflebeam, D. L. (eds.). *Evaluation Models: Viewpoints on Educational and Human Services Evaluation.* Boston, Mass.: Kluwer-Nijhoff, 1983.
Mentkowski, M., and Loacker, G. "Assessing and Validating the Outcomes of College." In P. T. Ewell (ed.), *Assessing Educational Outcomes.* New Directions for Institutional Research, no. 47. San Francisco: Jossey-Bass, 1985.
Merriam, S. B. *Case Study Research in Education: A Qualitative Approach.* San Francisco: Jossey-Bass, 1988.
Ory, J. C., and Parker, S. "Survey of Assessment Activities at Large Research Universities." Paper presented at the annual meeting of the American Educational Research Association, San Francisco, March 27–31, 1989.
Patton, M. Q. *Utilization-Focused Evaluation.* Beverly Hills, Calif.: Sage, 1978.
Patton, M. Q. *Qualitative Evaluation Methods.* Beverly Hills, Calif.: Sage, 1980.
Provost's Steering Committee on Assessment. *Assessment of Undergraduate Student Outcomes at UMC.* Columbia: University of Missouri, 1987.
Provus, M. M. *Discrepancy Evaluation.* Berkeley, Calif.: McCutchan, 1971.
Scriven, M. S. *The Methodologies of Evaluation.* AERA Monograph Series in Curriculum Evaluation, no. 1. Chicago: Rand McNally, 1967.
Scriven, M. S. "Goal-Free Evaluation." In E. R. House (ed.), *School Evaluation: The Politics and Process.* Berkeley, Calif.: McCutchan, 1973.
Shapiro, J. Z. "Evaluation Research and Educational Decision Making: A Review of the Literature." In J. C. Smart (ed.), *Higher Education: Handbook of Theory and Research.* Vol. 2. New York: Agathon Press, 1986.
Stake, R. E. (ed.). *Evaluating the Arts in Education: A Responsive Approach.* Columbus, Ohio: Merrill, 1975.
Stufflebeam, D., and others. *Educational Evaluation and Decision Making.* Itasca, Ill.: Peacock, 1971.
Tierney, W. G. "Ethnography: An Alternative Evaluation Methodology." *The Review of Higher Education,* 1985, *8* (2), 93–106.
Tyler, R. W. *Basic Principles of Curriculum and Instruction: Syllabus for Education 360.* Chicago: University of Chicago Press, 1949.
Weiss, C. H. "Evaluation for Decisions: Is Anybody There? Does Anybody Care?" *Evaluation Practice,* 1988, *9,* 5–19.

Clifton F. Conrad is professor of higher education at the University of Wisconsin-Madison.

David J. Eagan is a doctoral student in higher education, University of Wisconsin-Madison.

Universities that devise models to involve faculty in curricular change, building on commonalities among academic fields, can progress toward curricular coherence.

Seeking Coherence in the Curriculum

Joan S. Stark

Currently, reformers are urging that colleges develop "coherent curricula." While educators are responding to this challenge, the definition of curricular coherence remains unclear. Depending on one's perspective, achieving coherence may imply any or all of the following actions: requiring certain common studies of all students; changing and improving educational processes; increasing student involvement in learning; linking ideas from varied disciplines; or specifying and assessing intended student outcomes.

Particularly on complex campuses, political factors often seem to influence curricular change more strongly than educational factors do. Political influences dominate when proposals for educational improvement falter because faculty fail to agree on definitions and to select comprehensive models that can guide and evaluate programs. Colleges and universities that develop guiding models and clear definitions early in the process of curricular change are most likely to progress toward curricular coherence.

Research referred to in this paper was conducted under Office of Educational Research and Improvement (OERI) grant number G008690010, but the opinions expressed are those of the author.

Faculty involvement in candid discussions about why they endorse different views of coherence may mean the difference between transient curricular "tinkering" and educational improvement. The thesis of this chapter is that, early in the process of curricular change, considerable time and deliberate attention must be devoted to establishing and understanding the reasons why faculty so often seem to disagree. Such deliberate attention can ensure continued focus on educational considerations in curriculum plans and reduce the politicization of these plans.

To help educational factors remain paramount, universities must undertake these tasks:

1. Develop working definitions of curriculum and curricular coherence in order to organize change efforts and to guide evaluation.

2. Find educationally meaningful ways to bridge the disciplinary culture gaps on large campuses that hinder faculty communication and compete for students' time, attention, and loyalty. Since strongly socialized views of faculty are unlikely to change, coherence must build on a few goals of mutual importance to diverse groups.

3. Establish curricular change mechanisms that also expand faculty members' alternatives in course planning and teaching. The persistent search for coherence, involving shared teaching strategies among faculty from varied disciplinary cultures, may produce effective instructional change because the options are explored collegially and unobtrusively.

4. Communicate the college's view of coherence to students in broad institutional terms as well as specific educational goals and expectations at program and course levels. The fact that it is necessary to establish expectations at lower organizational levels should not absolve a large university from grappling with the meaning of coherence at an institutional level.

The Tale of a Committee

In order to develop these four points more fully, this chapter tells the tale of an imaginary faculty committee charged by the vice-president for academic affairs to develop a core course for lower-division students, a currently popular route to curricular reform that has been undertaken but failed to endure in times past (Cross, 1988). The story is told in two voices. The first voice (in regular type) is that of a narrator reporting typical campus committee discussions about curricular change. The second voice (in italics) is that of a committee member, acting as interpreter, who records observations and hypotheses about the process of curriculum change. These notes will be forwarded to the vice-president for academic affairs to inform future institutional planning. The perspectives expressed by both voices are drawn from interviews and discussions about course planning with faculty and students in varied disciplines and types of colleges and from two recent national surveys about educational beliefs, goals, and influences on course planning. These surveys included over 4,000 faculty in eight academic disciplines and ten professional fields (Stark and others, 1988; Stark and others, 1989). If the caricatures of faculty views in the committee narrative seem familiar, it is because they are based on known disciplinary differences in course planning.

The Vice-President's Charge

The Core Curriculum Committee has received a charge from the vice-president for academic affairs, a respected scholar who devotes thought to education as well as to budgets and personnel matters. The eloquent charge is lengthy, so we report only a few important points essential to our tale:

1. The vice-president hopes to understand and improve curricular change processes while responding to current reform initiatives. He notes that, although many colleges are focusing current change efforts at the institutional level, such global efforts may flounder at large universities. Thus, the vice-president urges the committee to proceed slowly and to demonstrate first a successful mechanism for cooperating to plan a single cross-disciplinary core course.

2. He asks that the committee be introspective, carefully recording and sharing observations about its experience that may subsequently inform change at the program or division level.

3. In the belief that clear and consistent definitions of curriculum and curricular coherence will underlie lasting change, the vice-president offers a tentative definition of curriculum to launch the committee's deliberations (Figure 1). He stresses that his view of curriculum as a plan provides a sense of dynamic purpose preferable to static views of curric-

Figure 1. The Vice-President's Tentative Definition of Curriculum

Curriculum is an academic plan incorporated in a course or a program of courses and thus includes the following:
- A selection of knowledge, skills, and attitudes to be learned
- A selection of subject matter in which to embed educational activities directed at acquiring the knowledge, skills, and attitudes
- A design for the educational activities, including organization of the subject matter
- A consideration of the previous backgrounds and skills of the learners
- A selection of materials, sources, tools, and settings to be used in the learning
- A method for evaluating the learning
- A system for considering and revising the plan in light of the evaluation.

Source: Stark and Lowther, 1986.

ulum as merely a set of courses or experiences. This definition of curriculum, or a similar one adopted by the committee, should encourage attention to important educational questions such as: What educational premises or purposes undergird the curricular plan? How can we ensure that the underlying educational goals remain paramount? What are the most important planning decisions to be made? Do we have the information needed to make these decisions carefully? How do we most effectively communicate the intent of the plan to students? How will various types of students experience the plan? Does it achieve the purposes we (and they) hope for them? What provisions have we automatically built in to evaluate and revise the plan?

Scene 1: The First Committee Meeting

Everyone comes prepared to make a strong contribution to the committee. Following the vice-president's example, the composition instructor (a nontenure-track faculty member, as is typical at large universities) provides the group with the tentative definitions of coherence and integration shown in Figure 2.

"The important distinction between coherence and integration," the composition instructor stresses, "is that coherence can exist in the abstract. But student interaction with the potentially coherent plan is necessary for integration to occur."

Not all committee members are content with these definitions, but they are anxious to set forth their own ideas on how the committee should proceed. Thus, they politely agree to accept them as working definitions to be revised later.

Several members have come with suggested organizing frameworks for the core course: The literature professor supplies a list of great books and important themes to be discovered in them. The history professor

Figure 2. One Instructor's Definitions

COHERENCE—A condition of logical consistency created by a set of well-understood principles.
CURRICULAR COHERENCE—A plan consistently expressing the purposes the faculty hopes to achieve and setting forth their best judgment about what methods will achieve these objectives.
INTEGRATION—The incorporation and unification of elements into a harmonious whole.
CURRICULAR INTEGRATION—A process occurring when students incorporate knowledge, behaviors, and attitudes included in the coherent curricular plan into their own lives. Student involvement and effort partially determine the extent to which the logically consistent plan is integrated by students.

Source: Stark, 1986.

provides a list of great historical events that students should surely review, preferably in chronological order. The biology professor suggests that the proposed interdisciplinary course be organized around concepts and principles of nature that people have discovered and include the historical and literary documentation of these discoveries. The fourth-year architecture student suggests that the course be one where students actively explore their world both in and out of the classroom. He proposes the title: "Discovering Our Cultural and Technical Environment."

Obviously frustrated, the nursing professor submits her belief that curriculum development should proceed more systematically than has yet been proposed, beginning with a clear list of learning goals. The tentatively accepted definition of coherence (to which she personally subscribes) will require knowing faculty intentions and how to link educational activities to them. Thus, she suggests that each member of the committee write down the most essential goal, aim, or objective to be achieved by the course.

Although the literature professor protests against writing detailed educational objectives without knowing students' personal needs, the group agrees to give the exercise a try. Here is what each writes as his or her most important overall course goal:

- Teach students to think effectively (biology and nursing professors)
- Learn ways to inquire into truth (composition instructor)
- Transmit the great ideas humans have generated (history professor)
- Clarify values and find personal enrichment (literature professor)
- Build a foundation for the future, learn to think effectively in a future professional role, and make the world a better place to live in (architecture student).

These widely divergent aims for the proposed course generate intense discussion. The composition instructor notes that the group's views are similar to those of faculty representing these disciplines generally. In a larger group, however, about half the faculty would endorse teaching effective thinking as their primary purpose (Stark and others, 1989).

The architecture student promptly challenges the group. "If so many professors espouse effective thinking as a primary goal, they must assume it can be taught by lecturing," he says. "Just how is not apparent to uninitiated students who sit passively in lectures, hour after hour."

"We are certainly not pursuing our agenda very systematically," says the biology professor, attempting to forestall a student attack on teaching competence. "But our student member is right; we should decide what the format for the course will be. Who will do the lectures? Will we have discussion groups and some field experiences?"

Since all committee members are now talking at once, we tune out briefly while the observer records notes for the vice-president.

1. Faculty who have been educated in different disciplines espouse dif-

ferent primary educational purposes, which may provoke intense arguments. Time spent recognizing and understanding the reasons for these arguments early in curricular deliberations may facilitate progress later. After discussing their varying beliefs about educational purpose, committee members agreed to remember that future disagreements may stem from these beliefs rather than from personal animosities or competition for curricular turf.

2. When planning an introductory course, most faculty members first select the content. About 15 percent spend some time thinking about the course objectives or aims; another 15 percent think first about student characteristics and preparation. A few begin by choosing course format and activities. Most probably move back and forth among objectives, content, and selection of activities. An interdisciplinary group, lacking common ground for selecting content, may move quickly to discuss specific teaching activities rather than persist in discussing basic purposes.

Scene 2: The First Confrontation

As we return to the committee meeting, the discussion still centers on instructional activities. Each faculty member campaigns for a favorite teaching method. The literature and composition teachers feel that participatory discussion groups are the best format. Such methods, they claim, engage students with the material, build their self-assurance, and allow them to be creative and to develop independence—in short, they encourage active learning. The biology and history professors are less comfortable with this form. "After all," they say, "this course is being created in response to criticisms that our students lack cultural literacy; they aren't learning enough important facts, principles, and concepts in the general education program. We must organize the material for the students so they will be clear about what important ideas they are to learn. The bad reputation of lectures is unmerited; they are definitely needed, particularly when there will be no single textbook to rely on."

Citing as models the architecture design studio and clinical training in social work, the student speculates that students may learn more when forced to experience situations they may encounter in their planned careers. "Also better for investment, involvement, engagement, or whatever it might be called," the student says. "But I'm not sure that this is true for all of my fellow students. Perhaps it depends on the students' preferred style of learning and how firm a sense of a future profession he or she has developed."

"For beginning students, it surely is a *faculty* responsibility," replies the history professor, "to provide some organizing framework, such as a set of historical phenomena to be explained or a chronological development of human progress. That, of course, is exactly the reason why my lectures are popular—because I organize the material for students. I always get good student evaluations on organization and clarity."

"Well, at least I know who invented those silly questions about organization and clarity on the teaching evaluations," says the composition instructor. "In my field, the organizing framework is the spirit of inquiry, the search for truth, and the creation of understanding out of chaos. I wouldn't presume to lecture to students. They must engage in seeking meaning and order for themselves."

To this, the biology professor responds "While I certainly would not wish to preclude others from using the scientific method, I must challenge your assertion that you 'search for truth' in teaching writing. You have implied that your field has no concepts, principles, or generalizations that are scientifically deduced and passed on to students!! Writing, however important, is merely a basic skill to be taught and certainly not a mode of inquiry."

The nursing professor reminds the group of its pact to try to transcend disagreements that result from strong disciplinary socialization. For the moment, the biology professor will have none of it. "You professional school faculty," he says accusingly to the nursing professor, "can distance yourselves from such discussions since you are subservient to your specialized accrediting agencies. All you think about is technical job-related skills to meet requirements for state board examinations. You are interested in training students, not in teaching them to think."

It is time fade out. . . .

Interim Events

Before their next meeting, the committee members receive information about how various professors characterize the fields they teach. For example, they learn that 90 percent of biology and nursing professors believe their fields consist of organized and interrelated bodies of knowledge to be taught, but less than 50 percent of literature faculty view their field in this way. Literature professors more often (70 percent) view their discipline as an interrelated set of values, as a group of individuals with a common interest in trying to understand the world. About two thirds (over 60 percent) of faculty in all the fields represented on the committee believe their discipline can be characterized as a "mode of inquiry," but they define this search for truth in quite different ways. This information helps committee members to understand the reasons for their acrimony (Stark and others, 1989).

3. Achieving agreement about course format and learning activities may not be much easier than grappling with educational purposes. For different fields, the typical content arrangement or type of presentation seems fairly well fixed. For example, instructors in biology rather commonly organize their teaching according to concepts and principles; historians frequently organize materials chronologically; and literature professors, depending on class preparation, choose themes they believe will stimulate personal growth. Some faculty members in all fields, often those with backgrounds in education, build on stated course objectives.

The committee also reviews a report asserting that the gap in educational purposes between liberal arts faculty and professional program faculty may not be as great as their outburst implied. The report suggests that faculty can build rapport by discussing mutually valued outcomes, such as communication skills, capacity for leadership, effective thinking, and others (Stark and Lowther, 1988).

4. *Perhaps the reason the core course continues to be reinvented with so little lasting success is that the attempt at consensus provokes a backlash that destroys good intention and colleagueship very quickly. While it is difficult to make such conflicts educationally productive, greater persistence and patience may be necessary as a deliberate strategy in curricular change when diverse cultures meet (Graff, 1988).*

5. *Better understanding of discipline-based diversity leads to the following untested hypotheses about achieving curricular change:*

If the goal is to increase faculty members' understanding of each other's work and/or to expose them to new teaching alternatives, establish a very diverse group, provide a long time frame, and insist that open discussion continue, using a mediator if needed.

If the goal is to adopt curricular changes quickly (or it doesn't matter whether the new programs endure), involve people from closely related fields or flexible faculty known to be willing to depart from disciplinary mainstreams. Time will be gained but change may be less enduring.

6. *Since faculty members do not regularly read educational studies outside of their disciplinary journals, an important committee member is a "translator" who can bring results of credible educational and psychological research to colleagues. The characteristics of translators and how individual faculty members can begin to assume this role are not clear but merit exploration.*

Scene 3: Finding Some Common Ground

As a subsequent committee meeting opens, the literature professor suggests that the group talk about the anticipated characteristics of students in this course and how their preparation will influence the plan. She reemphasizes the sense of discomfort she felt in attempting to write course aims without knowing more about student interests.

All committee members agree that student preparation, background, and expected effort are of consequence, but they express pessimism about obtaining information in time for advance planning or for guiding faculty members in the effective use of this information. They find that currently they cannot locate background information about their students even after classes have begun unless they collect it themselves.

7. *Improved knowledge of student characteristics is viewed as essential by most faculty as they plan courses. A separate committee should be established to explore what student information college teachers might find helpful and how it may be used in course planning. In a computer age, when accreditors, state boards, and testing services are demanding or encouraging new devices for assessing student learning, a campus should set a high priority on devising effective ways to use existing entry-level pretest information to improve course planning and teaching.*

8. *Since learning depends on integrating new knowledge with old, measures of the learning strategies students possess and those they adopt during a course are needed to help them know where they should be headed and how to get there (Pintrich and others, 1988).*

Having developed a common ground concerning the importance of student characteristics in planning, the committee moves on to a new topic. How may course goals best be conveyed to students? After discussion, the following points are added to the vice-president's list:

9. *When instructors tell students how they organize course concepts in their own minds and when they suggest appropriate strategies for learning, students not only learn more subject content; they also improve their learning strategies (McKeachie, Pintrich, Lin, and Smith, 1986).*

10. *Course syllabi may not fulfill their potential as communication devices. Syllabi for introductory courses generally tell students about assignments, grading, and other course logistics; they less frequently describe the instructor's rationale for selecting and arranging course material. Further, syllabi seldom relate a course to the broader educational goals and objectives of the sponsoring program or college. To encourage faculty to communicate course goals and to convey a sense of coherence to students, the committee recommends faculty discussions of comprehensive frameworks for syllabi (Lowther, Stark, and Martens, 1988).*

Scene 4: Assessing Involvement

Some weeks later, committee discussions are proceeding more smoothly.

"How will we know if the students are involved in their learning?" asks the literature professor at the start of a meeting. "You will recall our earlier discussion implying that instructors can write a curricular plan that appears coherent. But, until you have shown that it helps the students learn more and better, you can't say you have either genuine curricular coherence or integration."

"Faculty report that they observe students in ways based more on intuition and experience than on any systematic plan," says the composition instructor. "For example, over 90 percent of faculty teaching introductory courses say they watch students' faces, observe patterns of participation in class discussions, and check attendance as ways of assuring themselves that students are involved. More than 60 percent view completed assignments, examination results, after-class discussions, and office visits as additional indicators."

11. Faculty members who insist on systematic or proven methods in their scholarly work too often use only ad hoc and subjective methods of knowing whether students are engaged in learning. After discussing the importance of faculty awareness of levels of student involvement, the committee recommends that faculty be encouraged to use a handbook by Cross and Angelo (1988) entitled Classroom Assessment Techniques: A Handbook for Faculty.

12. The committee members, regardless of discipline, endorse an important educational principle and two corollaries:

Principle: The more ways faculty can find to communicate their educational intentions to students, the better.

Corollary 1: If faculty wish to communicate well, then the more they know about students the better.

Corollary 2: The more ways faculty can get systematic feedback about student learning, the better will be their curricular planning.

Scene 5: Unifying Themes for Progress

The communication corollaries—paraphrased by one committee member as "understanding students, helping students to understand our purposes and processes, and learning to understand whether they understand"—provides a unifying theme for the committee. This emphasis helps them transcend their initial disciplinary differences. They agree that *each* of their diverse perspectives is needed by students. Sharing their disagreements has helped them understand how important it is to share these same views with students in reasoned discourse. In this opportunity, they conclude, lies the real potential of the core course. While distribution requirements depend on separate exposure to many subjects and points of view, a core course can purposely organize differing views so they become obvious and meaningful to students.

As we leave our committee to its work, the members are placing items on their future agenda and that of the vice-president. Despite the productive agreements and smoother process they have achieved, they still face decisions about organizing mechanisms for the course. Here are three of the key issues that have emerged:

1. Survey findings show that, in introductory courses, very few faculty give much attention to mode of inquiry, to the research methods of

their field. Why? Is it difficult or impossible to share with students how we have come to know what we know? To what extent should we and can we deliberately expose beginning students to the research methods of our various fields?

2. Although faculty cite effective thinking as a major goal, we must return to the challenge posed by the student member of the committee: How does the way in which we teach connect to students learning to think effectively? How will we define and measure effective thinking in each field or in an interdisciplinary course?

3. To foster knowledge integration by students, we must consider at least two important dimensions: the extent to which ideas are conceptually related and the extent to which related ideas are studied in a close time frame. Does the advantage of a core course lie in the purposeful juxtaposition of one of these dimensions or in both? Are there other dimensions that could be examined that promise improved integration?

Finally, the committee is working on a preamble to its report to the vice-president. The first draft reads like this:

> In order to develop a more coherent curriculum, promote integrated student learning, and ensure successful assessment of our educational program, we hereby declare that the faculty members in a large university need not form a perfect union. They need not change their diverse educational views or attempt to recast them in the same mold. Faculty must, however, spend considerable time understanding their differences and melding their diverse viewpoints in ways that benefit students. These understanding and melding processes differ from the political tradeoffs so typical of most curriculum committee efforts. Curriculum committee meetings must begin with discussions of fundamental educational principles and persist to explore fully the reasons for diversity. The process must accommodate diversity by building on commonly accepted themes that form the essential basis of education.
>
> Whatever criticisms we initially had of the national reform movement, we must admit that it has brought us to the brink of progress. Your leadership and generous support for the committee's work have enabled us to pursue our discussions to the point of transcending our inevitable initial disagreements. Using our observations, we now request that you take the next step of extending this discussion to others in the university, decisively and persistently, with full awareness of the dangers of becoming mired in the swamp of faculty vulnerability as our colleagues expose their varied educational beliefs and strategies. We sense the need for a spirit of community, but we think it unlikely that everyone at a large university can become one big happy family. Nevertheless, conscious melding of varied perspectives into an educational plan may help us to link educational processes and outcomes more closely. The temptation to

return to a system of political tradeoffs must be firmly resisted when it occurs. As we have contemplated an expanded process, we have found the following statement useful as a guide: "It is important that professors talk among themselves, but it is more important that students get a sense of what is at issue in the cultural controversies on campus" (Graff, 1988).

References

Cross, K. P. "In Search of Zippers." *AAHE Bulletin*, 1988, *40* (10), 3–7.
Cross, K. P., and Angelo, T. A. *Classroom Assessment Techniques: A Handbook for Faculty*. Ann Arbor: National Center for Research to Improve Postsecondary Teaching and Learning, University of Michigan, 1988.
Graff, G. "Conflicts over the Curriculum Are Here to Stay; They Should Be Made Educationally Productive." *Chronicle of Higher Education*, 1988, *34* (23), A48.
Lowther, M. A., Stark, J. S., and Martens, G. *Course Syllabus Guide*. Ann Arbor: National Center for Research to Improve Postsecondary Teaching and Learning, University of Michigan, 1988.
McKeachie, W. J., Pintrich, P. R., Lin, Y., and Smith, D.A.F. *Teaching and Learning in the College Classroom: A Review of the Research Literature*. Ann Arbor: National Center for Research to Improve Postsecondary Teaching and Learning, University of Michigan, 1986.
Pintrich, P. R., and others. *Motivated Strategies for Learning Questionnaire (MSLQ)*. (Rev. ed.) Ann Arbor: National Center for Research to Improve Postsecondary Teaching and Learning, University of Michigan, 1988.
Stark, J. S. "On Defining Coherence and Integrity in the Curriculum." *Research in Higher Education*, 1986, *24* (4), 433–436.
Stark, J. S., and Lowther, M. A. *Designing the Learning Plan: A Review of Research and Theory Related to College Curricula*. Ann Arbor: National Center for Research to Improve Postsecondary Teaching and Learning, University of Michigan, 1986.
Stark, J. S., and Lowther, M. A. *Strengthening the Ties That Bind: Integrating Undergraduate Liberal and Professional Study*. Ann Arbor: National Center for Research to Improve Postsecondary Teaching and Learning, University of Michigan, 1988.
Stark, J. S., and others. *Reflections on Course Planning: Faculty and Students Consider Influences and Goals*. Ann Arbor: National Center for Research to Improve Postsecondary Teaching and Learning, University of Michigan, 1988.
Stark, J. S., and others. *Planning Introductory Courses: Technical Report*. Number 88-A-004-0. Ann Arbor: National Center for Research to Improve Postsecondary Teaching and Learning, University of Michigan, 1989.

Joan S. Stark is professor of higher education and director of the National Center for Research to Improve Postsecondary Teaching and Learning at the University of Michigan.

Future-directed liberal education that will prepare students for effective living is the major challenge for higher education today.

Undergraduate Curriculum 2000

Arthur Levine

Recently I have read many college curriculum reports. One that recently came over the transom included the following:

> One fact . . . is becoming more and more obvious every day. The American public is not satisfied with the present course of education. . . . And the great objection is that it is not sufficiently modern and comprehensive to meet the exigencies of the age and the country in which we live. . . . The complaint is . . . that, while everything is on the advance, our colleges are stationary or, if not quite stationary, that they are in danger of being left far behind in the rapid march of improvement.

The report went on to list a number of pointed questions about the state of undergraduate education: Why do colleges pay so little attention to civic and technological education? Why does the typical curriculum have such little regard for foreign languages, considering America's growing international ties? Why should young people planning on careers in business have to study a dead liberal arts core? The report said that the old arguments for maintaining the curriculum as is do not work any longer. It is not enough to say that the current curriculum worked for past generations. It is not enough to say that it teaches lifelong skills such as writing and speaking. The report concluded that, if colleges do not update their programs "to meet the public demand or if they choose not to do it," other institutions will.

What I read was not the American Association of Colleges report, nor the National Institute on Education report, nor Former Secretary of Education Bennett's report, nor any other familiar document. The report was written by the Amherst faculty in 1827 when Andrew Jackson was a candidate for president of the United States. It was an era much like the present. America was changing quickly and broadly; it was undergoing a transformation. A comfortable homogeneity was giving way to very real differences in people, institutions, and beliefs. Nationally, it was a time in which the economy was turbulent and technological revolution was sweeping the nation. Old industries were dying and new industries were booming. Demographics were shifting dramatically. The population was moving south and west. The number of young people was decreasing, and the number of older adults was rising. It was a time in which a large number of immigrants with little formal education were entering the country. Religious fundamentalism was experiencing a revival. Social institutions—church, family, and media—were being transformed. The accent was on shrinking the size and influence of the federal government. Last but not least, the president of the United States would soon be a popular two-term Westerner committed to cutting the national debt, increasing national defense, and enhancing thrift in government.

It was also a time in which higher education faced challenges like those faced today: Enrollments were falling, financial pressures were mounting, colleges were seeing more and more nontraditional students—poor people, some minorities, more adults. Competition from other educators—proprietary schools, apprenticeships, and industry—was increasing. Public confidence in higher education was diminishing. The journals of the era reported declining faculty morale, and there was high turnover in college presidencies. Colleges were being pressed to add new subjects, questioned about existing pedagogies, and doubted about the value of the liberal arts.

The colleges of that era reacted in much the same fashion as today's colleges. First, they underwent a crisis of purpose. Then they undertook a searching self-examination. Next, they issued reports that suggested varied and conflicting approaches to reform. Brown University prepared a report like the recent National Institute of Education (1984) document; students, the report said, ought to be more *involved in learning;* this involvement would lead to improvement. Amherst issued a statement like the Association of American Colleges' (1985) report on integrity in the college curriculum with a call for updating the liberal arts. Meanwhile, Yale, like Secretary of Education Bennett (1984), issued a call to reinstate the dead curriculum of the past.

In the aftermath of this flurry of activity, there was a great deal of innovation and experimentation. New subjects, such as science and modern languages, were added to the curriculum. New instructional methods and new technologies—such as seminars and blackboards—were tried. New degrees were offered; bachelor of philosophy; master of arts; doctoral degrees; degrees for women (since women could not be given the same degrees that men were awarded)—Sister of the arts, mistress of arts. Curriculum elements that had never appeared in higher education before were adopted—majors, minors, new grading systems—and colleges were reorganized into schools, departments, and disciplines. New missions were developed; research and services were added to religious training and teaching.

Under these new conditions, some institutions, even well-established ones, failed. Others, some unknown, emerged as national flagships. By the first decade of the twentieth century, the soul-searching had ended. The extraordinary climate for innovation waned. A new consensus was reached about higher education, its mission, subject matters, teaching methods, students, and all the rest. A new paradigm for undergraduate education had emerged.

Lessons from the Past

Three lessons from this past era stand out.

Impact of Social Change. The first lesson is that large-scale social change has a substantial impact on curriculum. We are now living through a period of profound demographic, economic, geographical, and technological change. When a society changes quickly or dramatically, it tends to leave behind all social institutions, colleges and universities included. A period of readjustment is required; it takes time for these institutions to catch up.

Predicting the needs of a society in motion is little more than a guessing game. To describe our society in the twenty-first century is to write science fiction. Which changes will be the most important and in what combination—the movement from an industrial/agrarian economy to one based on services/technologies, the globalization of our society, the changes in size and ethnicity of our population, or the development of yet-unknown technologies? How do universities respond to such changes?

We can name periods of profound change only in retrospect. During the 1830s, 1840s, and 1850s, people did not wake up in the morning and say, "Eureka! The reason that the old rules seem to be falling away and that values seem to be blurred is because we are living through the industrial revolution." No, they were confused, uncertain, even floundering. Not until the 1890s did the name "industrial revolution" stick; only then could this era begin to be understood. Similarly, from the 1830s through the 1850s higher education sought to develop a new curriculum paradigm to meet the needs of a new society. It took decades of experimentation to make the match. In the waning years of the twentieth century and the early portion of the twenty-first, such a match is likely to occur again.

Mistakes to Avoid. The second lesson is that there are mistakes to be avoided in the years ahead. One mistake is self-deprecation. Universities do not deserve to be crucified over the condition of education. That happened in the 1830s and 1840s, and it is happening now. Much of what was then and is now perceived as curricular disarray was a reflection of the times. Our universities are the victims, not the villains. They do not merit the abuse that is being heaped on them by the Department of Education, which ought to know better. We do not deserve the self-doubt that we have treated ourselves to lately. We should know better. Although the challenges of the twenty-first century are large, American higher education has a strong tradition of excellence and a record of rising to new challenges. We need to recognize both things: the need for change and the standard of quality we have.

Another mistake is attempting to recapture higher education's nostalgically remembered past. Over the last several years, a steady stream of books, reports, and pronouncements about higher education have done precisely that. Allan Bloom (1987) is the name most closely associated with this approach. The Yale faculty suggested the same tack in 1828. Even a casual reading of higher education history, however, shows that there was no golden era; the problems critics bemoan today have been perennial, varying over the years only in magnitude. Harking back to curricula that existed yesterday in order to prepare ourselves for what lies ahead does not make sense.

One more mistake that colleges made in the pre-Civil War years was adopting shortsighted curricular survival strategies. One might be called "drift" and the other "hunkering down." Drift occurs when a college simply turns its curriculum over to the marketplace, selling its educational authority to the highest bidder. This confuses standards with diversity. The colleges that adopted drift before the Civil War turned their curricula into "junkyards"—incoherent programs composed of an assortment of inconsistent odds and ends. The problems with a junkyard curriculum, beyond the real lack of educational merit, are several: First, a junkyard curriculum is expensive, far more so than a leaner, more carefully thought-out program. Second, a junkyard curriculum encourages mediocrity. Weak programs drain potentially strong programs of the resources required for good quality. Third, a junkyard does not attract students. They see the junkyard curriculum as half empty rather than half full.

Hunkering down is a strategy that moves in the opposite direction. During the industrial revolution, some schools just did nothing; they stuck tenaciously to a curriculum that had become dated and less useful. Such hunkering down has terribly negative effects on institutions. First, the emphasis changes from leadership to management. Second, the hunkering down permeates an entire institution, with everyone trying to hold onto his or her own turf. It divides department from department, individual from individual. Whatever it is that makes up academic community just dies. Not only is there no leadership, there is no followership. "Me" predominates. As a result, tough decisions are not made—decisions to strengthen a good area, decisions to eliminate a weak one. When budget cuts are necessary, they are likely to be made across the board with a net leveling of the entire institution. In short, institutions that hunker down trade quality for longevity. The irony is that it does not work. Hunkering down can only occur under two circumstances—when the problems are short term and when conditions are as bad as they are going to get. Neither is true today.

To summarize, universities need to avoid four mistakes that higher education has adopted in periods like the present: We cannot be self-abusive, we cannot seek the nostalgic rosy answers of the past, we cannot punt by turning decisions over to the marketplace, and we cannot remain vital by not acting.

Successes to Emulate. The third lesson consists of the successes that occurred during the pre-Civil War era—namely, the flagship schools that emerged. These schools were, for the most part, institutions with bold missions and vibrant educational programs that became models for other colleges. They were institutions like Nashville, Brown, Union, Harvard, the land-grant colleges, Cornell, Wisconsin, and Johns Hopkins. What these colleges had in common was a clearly defined institutional mission. We might call this common characteristic a "commitment to focus." Each mission was unique, but all these institutions had curricula that mirrored their mission. They had programs that responded to the educational needs of the times. Thus, they attracted more students when the overall number of students was shrinking. They garnered resources when the economy was turbulent. They attracted national recognition when education was declining as a national priority. For them, resources followed programming, not the other way around. In short, the lesson of the flagship institution is that educational vision is the best remedy for the challenges that face us today.

Challenges and Strategies for Today's Institutions

This is a very special moment in higher education. Higher education is confused and blurred; colleges and universities are uncertain about the problems that afflict them and how to respond to them. The institutional hierarchy is less stable than it has been at any time since World War II. In the next few years, we will see well-known institutions diminish in quality due to mistakes and inaction. We will see institutions less well known emerge as national models.

The challenge is to recognize, first, the need to think in terms of education—not to succumb to the bodies-and-bucks mentality that pervades higher education today. Second, we need to define what it means to be an educated person. What skills and knowledge do all people need in order to live in our society in the years ahead? Third, we need to recognize that students require an education that will give them the traditional preparation colleges have given: the knowledge to understand the world in which they live and the skills to live in that world in a socially beneficial and autonomous fashion.

Let me describe how we might accomplish this. What I suggest may sound suspiciously like a curriculum revival in the liberal arts. Well, it is.

Over the past several years, we have been treated to a sea of reports on undergraduate education with opposing diagnoses and an ocean of conflicting recommendations. If there is one theme they share, it is the clarion call for renewal of the liberal arts.

I think the reason is simple. The liberal arts respond well to what ails us today: the need to enhance student skills, the need to improve communication among people in an era of self-concern; the need to prepare students for life in a world in transition, for a hard and ceaselessly changing job market, for a world in which values and beliefs are confused and uncertain, and for a global society in which the margin for error has become paper thin.

The New Curriculum

A curriculum for the twenty-first century will need to educate students in the two languages all people must speak to live in this country—words and numbers. We need to teach students about the common human agenda—human heritage, science and technology, global perspectives, ethics and values, social institutions and all the rest—no matter what their major is. We need to provide students with education that will prepare them for careers—internships, counseling, practical minors, solid majors that are up to date and meet the needs of today's world. Students also need transitional skills. Throughout their lives, they will live in an age of enormous change; in such times, a particular set of skills is required. We might call them the three C's: critical thinking skills—analysis, synthesis, problem solving, questioning to help one sift and separate the important from the irrelevant; continuous learning—the ability to learn throughout one's life as the half-life of knowledge grows shorter and shorter; and creativity—fluency in thinking, the ability to discover new answers and new questions as one proceeds through life.

Finally, for students to develop the personal attributes required in a transitional society, they need an education that will give them a sense of efficacy—a belief that what they do matters. Today's students do not believe that. "Life is short, we can't make a difference anyway—why bother?" one young honors student told me recently, and 90 percent of his peers in the room agreed.

Students need an education that will give them a sense of responsibility. At the end of each year at Bradford, we ask freshmen to write an essay about the year just past and about their plans for the future. One young woman said that she wanted to be a chief executive officer of a multinational corporation, a U.S. senator, to serve at a foundation that gave scholarships to higher education, and to work on nuclear arms control. I asked what she needed out of college to achieve these things. She said, "A killer instinct." I pointed out the obvious altruism inherent in working on nuclear arms control. She responded incredulously that, if there were a nuclear war, she would not get to be a CEO of a multinational corporation. Altruism had no place in her thinking. We need to do better.

Students need an education that will give them hope. I was speaking with a junior high school group on my return from a trip to Japan. One student asked, "Did you go to Hiroshima?" I said that I had. She asked, "Will there be another nuclear war?" I asked the group to vote. Two out of three said they would definitely be or were likely to be in a nuclear war. We need to do better in the teaching of hope.

Many of our students graduate from college without a sense of altruism or hope. We can teach these things in the classroom. General education is, for example, the story of humankind's collective hopes, responsibilities, and achievements. But we can also teach these things outside the classroom—through cocurricular activities, awards, speaker series, service activities, financial aid requirements, orientation and graduation activities, and more.

This is the curricular agenda facing higher education today. The answer will not be found by merely dressing up the problems currently plaguing most universities. Over the decades ahead, there will be enormous pressure on universities to move from an emphasis on teaching to an emphasis on learning. This is no small change, but amounts to a transformation in university education. There will be increasing pressure on universities to move from an emphasis on process—courses and credits—to an emphasis on outcomes. This, too, has the potential to alter higher education dramatically.

To confront these pressures, we will need an ongoing reexamination of the disciplines, the allocation of faculty, and the ways that we organize knowledge. In the decades ahead, some of the existing patterns will become old and less useful; new fields, specialties, and knowledge will become essential. There will also be the press of new pedagogies and more effective ways to learn. We are on the verge of a revolution in understanding how the brain works. There will be the impact of new technologies, new educational needs—will the four-year undergraduate college continue to make any sense?—and new educators. There may be more to learn about liberal education in the next few years from the Betty Crocker Institute and the army than from a highly selective liberal arts college. In short, the decades ahead will be a time for experimentation and bold thought.

In his biography, Henry Adams (1918) wrote about his undergraduate education that he had attended Harvard in the nineteenth century while the college was offering an eighteenth-century curriculum and the nation was plunging into the twentieth. The challenge to higher education today is to develop a curriculum that can move with the nation—and the world—as we plunge into the twenty-first century.

References

Adams, H. *The Education of Henry Adams.* Boston, Mass.: Houghton Mifflin, 1918.
Amherst Faculty Report. Amherst, Mass.: Amherst University, 1827.
Association of American Colleges. *Integrity in the College Curriculum: A Report to the Academic Community.* Washington, D.C.: Association of American Colleges, 1985.
Bennett, W. *To Reclaim a Legacy.* Washington, D.C.: National Endowment for the Humanities, 1984.
Bloom, A. *The Closing of the American Mind.* New York: Simon and Schuster, 1987.
National Institute of Education. *Involvement in Learning.* Washington, D.C.: U.S. Government Printing Office, 1984.

Arthur Levine is president of Bradford College, Bradford, Massachusetts. In July 1989, he will become chair of the Institute for Educational Management and member of the senior faculty, Harvard Graduate School of Education.

APPENDIX
Framework for a Workshop on Good Practice in Undergraduate Education
Arthur W. Chickering

"Seven Principles for Good Practice in Undergraduate Education" (Chickering and Gamson, 1987) provided the foundation for a workshop on improving undergraduate education in a large university. This Appendix briefly discusses the seven principles and the workshop itself, held at the University of Minnesota, May 6, 1988.

Principle 1: Good Practice Encourages Student-Faculty Contact

> Frequent student-faculty contact in and out of classes is the most important factor in student motivation and involvement. Faculty concern helps students get through rough times and keep on working. Knowing a few faculty members well enhances students' intellectual commitment and encourages them to think about their own values and future plans (Chickering and Gamson, 1987, p. 4).

Research demonstrates that the single most powerful variable in a student's experience of higher education is significant contact with one or more faculty members. Many students describe this kind of relationship, when they have it, as equal in importance to the formative experiences with their parents. Frequent student-faculty contact in and out of class explains more of the variance in student development in college than any other single variable.

Principle 2: Good Practice Encourages Cooperation Among Students

> Learning is enhanced when it is more like a team effort than a solo race. Good learning, like good work, is collaborative and social, not competitive and isolated. Working with others often increases involvement in learning. Sharing one's own ideas and responding to others' reactions improves thinking and deepens understanding (p. 4).

The second most important variable for student development in college is student interaction with other students. These interactions with peer groups and individuals have a very powerful influence, in class and out of class. When learning is done collaboratively or when scheduling and curricular arrangements make it possible for students to share the same courses and get together around those courses outside of class, the educational power of their experience is increased dramatically. Conversely, when we have a highly competitive, dog-eat-dog environment where a high priority is placed on grading on a curve, we may get high performance on exams but little significant augmentation of working knowledge that lasts very long.

Principle 3: Good Practice Encourages Active Learning

> Learning is not a spectator sport. Students do not learn much just sitting in classes listening to teachers, memorizing prepackaged assignments, and spitting out answers. They must talk about what they are learning, write about it, relate it to

past experiences, and apply it to their daily lives. They must make what they learn part of themselves (p. 5).

This principle could be furthered by expanding on the kinds of opportunities that already exist and extending the active concept to a broader segment of the curriculum. To accomplish this, respected administrators must provide committed leadership and support. Staff development opportunities to assist faculty in developing practical strategies for active learning and alternative delivery systems are needed. These include departmental field retreats as well as collegiate forums for sharing experiences. A reward system for faculty for planning and implementing active learning approaches is important. Students themselves can be involved as discussion group leaders and peer tutors, and more modern equipment (audiovisual equipment, video cameras and recorders) should be available for student use independently and in the field. Student expectations for involvement in learning should be set early through introductory classes that emphasize laboratory-type problems.

Principle 4: Good Practice Gives Prompt Feedback

Knowing what you know and don't know focuses learning. Students need appropriate feedback on performance to benefit from courses. In getting started, students need help in assessing existing knowledge and competence. In classes, students need frequent opportunities to perform and to receive suggestions for improvement. At various points during college and at the end, students need chances to reflect on what they have learned, what they still need to know, and how to assess themselves (p. 5).

Students, like the rest of us, cannot really learn without feedback, no matter what it is. Evaluation in that sense is inseparable from learning; it is inseparable from behavior. One of the things that makes learning in concrete performance areas so highly motivated and enables us to sustain effort is the direct, unequivocal feedback these activities provide. If we are learning to play tennis, ski, hit a golf ball, perform on a musical instrument, or dance, we get feedback we cannot ignore. It is an integral part of the process that is not only motivating but also enables us to learn effectively. If you do not know how you are doing, it is hard to sustain motivation, and it is hard to know where best to invest time and energy. Learning is powerfully strengthened by feedback early in the semester when students get information about how they are doing, when there is substantive information about performance on a fairly continuous basis, both from faculty members and from other students, and when the results of examinations are talked about soon after the examination is given. How many courses discuss the results of the final exam with students, as a group or with each individual? It seldom happens. It is the most important feedback loop of the whole course, and we ignore it. In fact, students often get their grades and any substantive information after they are involved in something else. So our ability and our practices that have to do with continuous feedback leave much room for improvement.

Principle 5: Good Practice Emphasizes Time on Task

Time plus energy equals learning. There is no substitute for time on task. Learning to use one's time well is critical for students and professionals alike. Students need help in learning effective time management. Allocating realistic amounts of time means effective learning for students and effective teaching for faculty. How an institution defines time expectations for students, faculty, administrators, and other professional staff can establish the basis for high performance for all (p. 5).

It is obvious to say that you cannot learn without spending time and energy doing it. Yet it is amazing how infrequently we try to get that message across, how infrequently we make clear, when students are enrolling in a course or in a program, the time, energy, and activities required if they are going to learn anything.

The tough problem, the political problem and resource problem, is how you get faculty time and energy invested in teaching and in spending time with students in a high-powered research university. Unless the adviser-advisee ratio is changed, you are not going to improve academic advising. Unless there is more time invested in teaching in ways that encourage active learning, you are not going to improve the quality of education that goes on in classes. The reward system is an important part of that. Obviously, we need to find a way to recognize those faculty members who are good and who want to invest time and energy in advising, or are good and want to invest significant time and energy in high-quality teaching, and to give them some payoff. Unless these things can happen, rhetoric will be helpful but it will not have much impact on what is actually going on in the institution.

Principle 6: Good Practice Communicates High Expectations

> Expect more and you will get it. High expectations are important for everyone—for the poorly prepared, for those unwilling to exert themselves, and for the bright and well motivated. Expecting students to perform well becomes a self-fulfilling prophecy when teachers and institutions hold high expectations of themselves and make extra efforts (p. 6).

High expectations are critical. These include expectations of the level of intellectual competence and complexity at which students are going to operate, the difficulty level of the reading materials they are expected to handle, and the level of complexity of the field experiences and field problems that they are asked to deal with. Similarly, we need high expectations for ourselves in terms of the educational quality of our programs. We see the most dramatic examples of high expectations in some of the principals and superintendents that have turned around inner-city schools.

Principle 7: Good Practice Respects Diverse Talents and Ways of Learning

> There are many roads to learning. People bring different talents and styles of learning to college. Brilliant students in the seminar room may be all thumbs in the lab or art studio. Students rich in hands-on experience may not do so well with theory. Students need the opportunity to show their talents and learn in ways that work for them. Then they can be pushed to learn in new ways that do not come so easily (p. 6).

There are numerous conceptual frameworks that can help us think about individual differences. Until we find ways to recognize, respect, and respond to those individual differences, we are going to miss two thirds or three quarters of the students we are teaching. We cannot batch process students the way we thought we could when we were dealing with well-prepared traditional students who were coming to us from the top 10 or 20 percent of their high school classes, out of middle-class families with lots of books in the house. We not only have to find programmatic responses—mastery learning, contract learning, individualized majors, and so on—but we also must find ways to deal with individual differences in our classroom groups. The capacity for this is not inborn; there is an extensive body of literature and professional expertise to assist in this effort. It is critically important in our pluralistic culture that we not turn away from the importance of access to higher education. If we are to avoid a two-tier society, we have to help all segments of our society achieve significant learning and learn to function in a complex workplace.

The Workshop

Following opening remarks by the author about the principles, each participant responded to five questions concerning a principle of his or her choice:
1. What aspects of your institution *strengthen* the operation of this principle?
2. What aspects of your institution *weaken* the operation of this principle?
3. Can you give any examples of how this principle operates in your institution? Please consider courses, teaching, curriculum, student services, assessment, extracurricular activities.
4. How can we further implement this principle? What might be a "next step" for your department, college, or institution?
5. What resources and structures are needed to make this happen?

Subgroups established by principle then shared individual responses and discussed the implications for the University of Minnesota and for other participating institutions. Participants included faculty, administrators, professional support staff, and students from higher education institutions in the state. The workshop concluded with subgroup reports and some final remarks by the author.

Reference

Chickering, A. W., and Gamson, Z. F. "Seven Principles for Good Practice in Undergraduate Education." *AAHE Bulletin*, 1987, *39* (7), 2-7.

Arthur W. Chickering is Visiting Distinguished Professor, George Mason University, Fairfax, Virginia, and Distinguished Professor of Higher Education at Memphis State University.

Index

A

Academic Profile, 47
Academic program environment, and evaluation, 58-59
Action first, planning, 22
Adams, H., 84
Adelman, C., 36, 39
Administration, 12-13; and evaluation control, 55; leadership role of, 15-17; and pressures for change, 21
Aiken, W., 38, 39
Alliance for Undergraduate Education, 42-43
Allison, G., 19, 23
Alverno College, 2, 59
Alverno College Faculty, 2, 8, 59, 61
American College Testing College Outcomes Measures Project (ACT COMP), 59
Amherst Faculty Report, 77-78, 84
Angelo, T. A., 74, 76
Antioch University, 15
Arizona Plan, 58-59
Assessment, 51-52; projects, 47-48. *See also* Formative assessment; Research and assessment; Summative assessment
Association of American Colleges, 78, 84
Astin, A. W., 41, 48, 59, 60-61, 62
Ayala, F., Jr., 59, 60, 62

B

Baldridge, J. V., 12, 14, 17, 23
Banta, T. W., 2, 8, 52-53, 59, 61
Barriers, to excellence in undergraduate education, 4
Bebeau, M., 43, 48
Bednarz, D., 59, 61
Bennett, W., 12, 34, 39, 78, 84
Bentley, R. J., 67, 69, 71, 76
Bloom, A., 80, 84
Blumenthal, D., 18, 24
Bok, D., 12

Bomotti, S. S., 67, 76
Boyer, C. M., 2, 8, 58, 62
Boyer, E. L., 41, 48
Bradford College, 83
Breland, H., 29-30, 39
Brodigan, D., 30, 40
Brown University, 78, 81
Brubacher, J., 11, 24
Brunsson, N., 20, 24
Bunderson, C., 31, 39
Bush Collaboration Project, 42-43

C

Calvin, C., 46, 49
Center for Research on Undergraduate Education, 56
Change, institutional: buffering and coping with, 22-23; examples of, 2; facets of, 5-6
Chickering, A. W., 6, 8, 85-89
Civil Rights Restoration Act, 30, 39
Clinical Versus Statistical Prediction, 33, 40
Clugston, R., 19, 24
Cohen, M., 14, 16, 20, 24
Coherence, definition of, 68
College Outcome Measures Project, 47
Collins, T., 45, 48
A Commitment to Focus, 3-4, 7-8, 9-25, 37-38
Comprehensive evaluation, 56
Computers, and learning-disabled students, 45
Connoisseurship model, 58
Conrad, C. F., 17, 18, 21, 24, 52-53, 55, 56-59, 61
Consumer control, and higher education, 12
Context, Input, Process, Product (CIPP) model, 57-58
Control, in evaluation, 54-55
Conventional wisdom, and research and assessment, 33-35
Cook, T. D., 59, 61

89

Cooperation, among students, 85-86
Cooperative Assessment for Experiential Learning's Project, 38
Core Curriculum Committee, 67-76; assessing involvement in, 73-74; and finding common ground, 72-73; first confrontation of, 70-71; first meeting of, 68-70; interim events in, 71-72; and themes for progress, 74-76
Cornell University, 81
Crooks, T., 73, 76
Cross, K. P., 42, 48, 66, 74, 76
Curricular coherence, 65-76; committee for, 66-76; definition of, 68; and the vice-president's charge, 67-68
Curricular integration, definition of, 68
Curriculum: definition of, 67; development efforts, 43-44; of the future, 81-84; and lessons from the past, 77-81
Curriculum reform, 9-25; and characteristics of change, 11-14; implications of, 23; and institutional change, 10-11; leadership for, 14-19; management of, 20-23; models for change management and survival in, 19-20
Curtis, D. V., 12, 14, 17

D

Dean, leadership role of, 17
Decision-making model, 57-58
Defining Issues Test, 43, 47
Delbecq, A., 27, 39
Dental Ethical Sensitivity Test, 43
Department cultures, and curriculum reform, 18-19
Department of Education, 80
Dinham, S. M., 52, 56, 61
Disadvantaged students, student services for, 46
Doljanac, R., 73, 76
Donald, J. G., 42, 48
Dressel, P., 28, 39
Drift, as mistake in education, 80

E

Ecker, G., 12, 14, 17, 23
Eckert, R., 39

Economic survival, as source of change, 30-31
Edelman, M., 56, 61
Edgerton, R., 42, 49
Education Commission of the States, 2, 8
Educational Development Program, 42-43
Eisner, E. W., 58, 61
El-Khawas, E., 36, 40
Engen-Wedin, N., 45, 48
Ethics, teaching, in dentistry, 43-44
Evaluation, 51-63; challenge of, 52; emphasis, 58-59; focus and scope of, 55-56; formative, 54; involvement and control in, 54-55; and methods of measurement, 59-60; models, 56-58; purposes of, 53-54; summative, 54
Ewell, P. T., 2, 8, 36, 40, 53, 58, 61-62
Excellence: achieving, 51-63; elements of, 4-5
Expectations, high, and learning, 88

F

Factual foundation, as tactic for change, 36
Faculty, 12-13; and curricular coherence, 65-76; as entrepreneurs, 21-22; in the large university, 14
Feedback, and learning, 86-87
Finney, J. E., 2, 8
Fisher, H. S., 2, 8, 52-53, 61
Flexibility, and higher education, 12
Foley, W., 57-58, 62
Formative assessment, as tactic for change, 37
Formative evaluation, 54
Funded programs, as source of change, 29
Future-directed curriculum, 77-84

G

Gamson, Z. F., 6, 8, 85-89
Gaphart, W., 57-58, 62
Gardner, D. E., 57, 62
Geiger, R., 42, 49
Genthon, M., 67, 69, 71, 73, 76
Gluck, M. E., 18, 24
Goal-based model, 57
Goertz, M., 29-30, 40

Graduate Record Exam (GRE), 59
Graff, G., 72, 75-76
Grove City College v. *Bell*, 30, 40
Guba, E. G., 57, 60, 62

H

Hammond, R., 57-58, 62
Harvard University, 81
Havens, C. L., 67, 76
Hefferlin, J., 31-32, 40
Heiss, A., 28, 40
Hendel, D. D., 47, 49
Higher education: curricular history of, 79-81; curriculum for today, 81-82; future curriculum, 82-84; system, 12-13
Higher Education Commission (Tennessee), 2
Homons, G., 17, 24
Hope, and education, 83
Hrebiniek, L., 13, 24
Humanistic wisdom, and research and assessment, 32-33
Hunkering down, as mistake in education, 81
Hutchins, R., 31, 40

I

Implementation Task Force on Undergraduate Education, 4, 8
Improving undergraduate education: and curricular coherence, 65-76; and the curriculum of the future, 77-84; and curriculum reform, 9-25; and evaluation, 51-63; keys to, 4-5; and research and assessment, 27-40; research-based projects for, 41-49; workshop framework for, 85-89
Individual differences, and learning, 88
Inouye, D., 31, 39
Institutional renewal, as source of change, 31-32
Integration, definition of, 68
Involvement in Learning, 34-35, 40

J

Jacobi, M., 59, 60, 62
Johns Hopkins University, 81

Johnson, L., 29-30, 40
Junkyard curriculum, as mistake in education, 80

K

Kanter, R., 18-19, 24
Karabenick, S., 73, 76
Keeton, M. T., 28, 40
Keller, K., 3-4, 8, 10, 15, 24, 37-38, 40
Keller, R., 39
Kellogg Foundation, 44
Kerr, C., 13-14, 19, 24
Koch, L., 45, 49
Krueger, D. W., 59, 62

L

Large university, organizational characteristics of, 13-14
Leadership, for curriculum reform, 14-19
Learning, active, 86
Learning-disabled students, using computers with, 45
Legal mandates, as source of change, 30
Lin, Y., 42, 49, 73, 76
Lincoln, Y. S., 57, 60, 62
Lindblom, C., 19-20, 24
Lindquist, J., 18, 24
Litten, L., 30, 40
Loacker, G., 59, 62
Louis, K. S., 18, 20, 21-22, 24
Lowther, M. A., 67, 69, 71-73, 76

M

McClain, C. J., 59, 62
McKeachie, W. J., 42, 49, 73, 76
Madaus, G. F., 57, 62
Manns, C. L., 12, 24
March, J., 12, 14, 16, 19-20, 24
Margolis, W., 45, 48
Martens, G. G., 67, 69, 71, 73, 76
Mathematics, problem-solving strategies in, 44-45
Matross, R., 47, 49
MCAT, 59
Measurement, methods, 59-60
Meehl, P., 33, 40
Mentkowski, M., 59, 62

Merriam, S. B., 60, 62
Merriman, H., 57-58, 62
Miles, M., 20, 21, 24
Mills, P., 27, 39
Mingle, J. R., 2, 8
Minority students, group advising with, 46
Models: evaluation, 56-58; planning, 19-20
Molitor, J., 21-22, 24
Moore, W., 14, 24

N

National Commission on Excellence in Education, 29, 40
National Institute of Education, 78, 84
Naveh-Benjamin, M., 73, 76
Northeast Missouri State University, 59

O

Olsen, J., 14, 19-20, 24, 31, 39
Ory, J. C., 53, 62
Outcomes, and evaluation, 59

P

Parker, S., 53, 62
Patton, M. Q., 53, 56, 59, 62
Pava, C., 20, 24
Pechtel, B., 44, 49
Peters, T., 13, 24
Pfeffer, J., 14, 24
Pintrich, P. R., 42, 49, 73, 76
Plan for Focus: Commitment to Focus Advisory Task Force on Planning, 38, 40
Planning model. *See* Models, planning
Policy issues, as tactic for change, 37-38
Popular mandate, as source of change, 29-30
Price, L., 45, 48
Principles, for improving undergraduate education, 85-89
Programs, sound, as tactic for change, 38
Project Sunrise, 44

Projects, for improving undergraduate education, 41-49
Provost's Steering Committee on Assessment, 55, 62
Provus, M. M., 57, 62

Q

Qualitative measurement, 60
Quantitative measurement, 59-60

R

Reflection and celebration, opportunities for, 22
Reform movements, as source of change, 28
Reichardt, C. S., 59, 61
Research, classroom, 44-45
Research and assessment, 27-40; in the classroom, 44-45; role of, 32-35; as sources of educational change, 28-32; tactical uses of, 35-39
Research involvement, as tactic for change, 38-39
Research-based projects, for improving undergraduate education, 41-49
Resources, in the large university, 14
Responsibility, and education, 83
Responsive model, 57
Riecken, H., 17, 24
Riley, G. L., 12, 14, 17, 23
Rivas, M., 46, 49
Rosenblum, S., 21-22, 24
Rossman, J., 36, 40
Rudy, W., 11, 24
Ryan, M. P., 67, 69, 71, 76

S

Salancik, G., 14, 24
Schmitz, C., 46, 49
Scriven, M. S., 54, 57, 62
Self-deprecation, as mistake in education, 80
Senate Committee on Educational Policy (SCEP), 47
Shapiro, J. Z., 56-57, 62
Smith, D.A.F., 42, 49, 73, 76
Snow, C., 13, 24
Social change, impact of, on curriculum, 79-80

Sophomore Assessment Project, 47
Specific evaluation, 56
Stake, R. E., 55, 57, 62
Stark, J. S., 67-69, 71-73, 76
Stoto, M. A., 18, 24
Structural modifications, as source of change, 28-29
Student characteristics, and evaluation, 58-59
Student services projects, 45-46
Students: and cooperation, 85-86; disadvantaged, 46; in the large university, 13-14; learning-disabled, 45; minority, 46
Study Group on the Conditions of Excellence in American Higher Education, 34-35, 40
Stufflebeam, D. L., 57-58, 62
Sullivan, A. M., 42, 49
Sullivan, D., 30, 40
Summative assessment, as tactic for change, 36-37
Summative evaluation, 54

T

Taylor, B., 15, 25
Technical wisdom, and research and assessment, 32
Technological advance, as source of change, 31
Theme, for curriculum reform, 21
Tichy, N., 10, 25
Tierney, W. G., 60, 62
Time on task, and learning, 87
Title IX of the Education Amendments of 1972, 30, 40

Trow, M., 12, 25
Tyler, R. W., 57, 62

U

Undergraduate Research Opportunities, 42-43
Union College, 81
University. *See* Large university
University of Arizona, 42
University of California, 42
University of Minnesota, 3-4, 6-8, 16, 25, 52, 85; and projects for improving education, 41-49. *See also A Commitment to Focus*
University of Pittsburgh, 42
University of Tennessee at Knoxville, 2, 59

V

Vaill, P., 21, 25

W

Waterman, R., 13, 24
Weick, K., 14, 25
Weiss, C. H., 56, 62
Willingham, W. W., 38, 40
Wilson, R. F., 52-53, 57-58, 61
Wisconsin University, 81
Wisdom, and research and assessment, 32-35
Workshop, on good practice in undergraduate education, 85-89
Wren, P. A., 67, 69, 71, 76

Y

Yale University, 78